GYMNASTIC ACTIVITIES • DANCE • GAMES

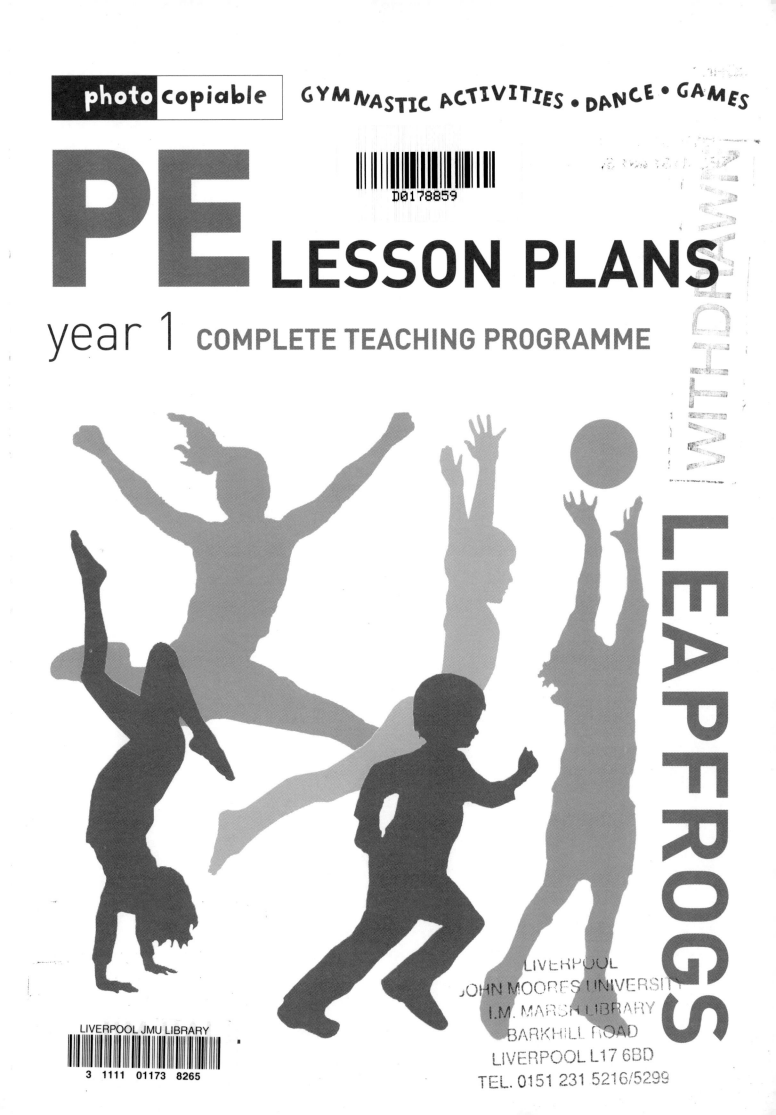

D0178859

PE LESSON PLANS

year 1 COMPLETE TEACHING PROGRAMME

WITHDRAWN

LEAPFROGS

Published in 2005 by A & C Black Publishers Ltd
37 Soho Square, London W1D 3QZ
www.acblack.com

ISBN 0 7136 7212 9

A CIP record for this book is available from the British Library.

Note: While every effort has been made to ensure that the content of this book is as technically accurate and as sound as possible, neither the author nor the publisher can accept responsibility for any injury or loss sustained as a result of the use of this material.

A & C Black uses paper produced with elemental chlorine-free pulp, harvested from managed sustainable forests.

Acknowledgements
Cover and inside design by Peter Bailey
Illustrations by Eleanor King

Typeset in 10pt DIN Regular.

Printed and bound in Great Britain by Martins the Printers, Berwick upon Tweed.

Contents

Introduction

Good lesson plans and a sense of staff unity regarding the 'Why?' 'What?' and 'How?' of Physical Education are essential to a successful programme with high standards and continuity from year to year. Included in this book is a year's worth of lesson plans and detailed accompanying notes to help with the 'Why?' 'What?' and 'How?' It is hoped that these user-friendly lesson plans and notes will also contribute to the development of a sense of staff-room togetherness in a belief in the value of, and a desire to apply good practice in, Physical Education.

A pupil's all-round educational development is at its most intense during the infant school years and Physical Education makes unique and valuable contributions to this.

○ **physical** development comes from lively participation in all the natural activities of running, jumping, landing, climbing, rolling, balancing, taking weight on to the hands, lifting and carrying light apparatus, chasing, dodging, and playing with a wide variety of games implements;

○ **social** development comes from sharing hall and playground space unselfishly with others, demonstrating to help others learn if called upon, watching and commenting appreciatively on others' performances, taking turns, and helping others to lift and carry apparatus;

○ **emotional** development comes from enjoying a sense of pleasure from participation in natural activities, feeling better about oneself after being praised for good work, and getting rid of surplus energy, which is normal in young, naturally active children. Such release is now denied to many young children whose lifestyles are becoming more sedentary and less physical;

○ **intellectual** development accompanies the gaining of knowledge and understanding about ways of moving and controlling our bodies. Children will begin to make judgements about themselves in the space being shared with others.

The stimulation of almost non-stop, vigorous and enjoyable activity should be the most important feature and aim of Physical Education, ideally inspired by enthusiastic teachers who value the subject. Working in a hall or playground with apparatus, wide spaces, rapidly moving pupils and safety and behaviour considerations to manage, is a problem, particularly for teachers with limited training in teaching Physical Education. This book aims to help teachers by providing information, ideas and practical help with planning, teaching and developing their Gymnastic Activities, Dance and Games lessons. It also aims to provide schools with suggestions for planning the content of their progressive programmes in these three activities.

Jim Hall
March 2005

Gymnastic Activities

Introduction to Gymnastic Activities

The Gymnastic Activities lesson includes varied floorwork on a clear floor, unimpeded by gymnastic apparatus, chairs, trolleys or a piano, followed by varied apparatus work that covers half to two-thirds of the lesson time. The apparatus will have been placed around the sides and ends of the hall, near to where it will be positioned and used in the lesson.

The focus is on the body and helping each pupil to move neatly with control and versatility. The lessons should also be physically demanding to develop strength and suppleness. Activities include the natural movements of running, jumping, landing, rolling, climbing, swinging, balancing, taking weight onto hands, bending, stretching and twisting. Performing these movements maintains and develops the body's capacity to use them. Traditional, popular gymnastic skills include rolls, handstands, cartwheels, headstands, rope climbing, circling on bars, balances on inverted benches and easy vaults on to and from a low box. Awareness of the variety and contrasts possible in movement and how to demonstrate them can be developed through experiencing different shapes, directions, levels, speeds and amounts of force, which can all be applied to enhance and progress a performance.

The naturalness and variety of what is being taught, children's enthusiasm for movement and their energy and capacity for hard work, and the high standards of performance that the majority can achieve all combine to make Gymnastic Activities lessons a valuable, exciting part of the Physical Education programme.

The following pages provide a scheme of work for Year 1 Gymnastic Activities. There is a lesson plan for each month and an accompanying page of explanatory notes, designed to help teachers and schools with ideas for lessons that are progressive and implement the NC requirements. The lessons usually run for four weeks to allow pupils to practise, repeat, learn, remember and develop the skills involved.

It is hoped that these pages also help to produce a sense of staff-room togetherness regarding the nature of good practice and high standards in teaching Gymnastic Activities lessons. Without this sense of unity among the teachers concerned, there is no continuity of expectations or programme and there will be a less than satisfactory level of achievement.

Why do we teach Gymnastic Activities?

○ Because it is the most active of all Physical Education activities. It exercises and develops all muscle groups and it stretches and bends all joints to their full range.
   We want our still-growing pupils to grow well.

○ Because it uses and develops skill in natural activities such as running, jumping, rolling, balancing, climbing, swinging, inverting, bending, stretching, arching and twisting in many challenging situations, on the floor and on apparatus. Self-control and body management are practised and developed, leading to good, confident, poised, controlled, versatile and safe movement in daily life.
   We want our pupils to move well.

○ Because the actions being practised are natural, improvement can be quick if enthusiastic pupils work hard. A pupil's regard for and attitude towards his or her physical self, particularly at primary school stage, is important to the development of self-image and to the value given to oneself.
   We want our pupils to feel self-confident and pleased with themselves.

○ Because pupils have to co-operate to share space safely and considerately with others, work together to lift, carry, place and use apparatus, take turns, demonstrate and be demonstrated to, the Gymnastic Activities lesson can develop an enhanced capacity for pleasant, co-operative social relationships.
   We want our pupils to work and get on well with others.

○ Because Gymnastic Activities provide opportunities for exciting, almost adventurous actions (particularly climbing, swinging, balancing, jumping and landing) and vigorous physical exercise – seldom experienced away from school – these lessons should be seen as antidotes to the increasingly inactive, sedentary and unhealthy lifestyles of many children.
   We want our pupils to be excited by these lessons and use them as outlets for their energy. We want them to believe that exercise is good for you; is good for your heart; and makes you feel and look better.

The Gymnastic Activities lesson plan

One answer to the question 'What do we teach in a Gymnastic Activities lesson?' might be 'All the natural actions and ways of moving of which the body is capable and which, if practised whole-heartedly and safely, ensure normal, healthy growth and physical development.'

It has been said that 'What you don't use, you lose.' Most pupils nowadays seldom use their natural capacity for vigorous running, jumping and landing from a height; rolling in different directions; balancing on a variety of body parts; upending to take their weight on their hands; gripping, climbing and swinging on a rope; hanging, swinging and circling on a bar; or whole body bending, stretching, arching and twisting. These natural movements and actions should be present in every Gymnastic Activities lesson, ensuring that pupils do not lose the ability to perform them and have their physical development diminished.

A class teacher's determination to inspire the class to use and not lose their natural physicality can be strengthened by looking at the cars queuing as near to the school exit as possible, ready to transport children home – with the minimum of walking – to their after-school, house-bound, sedentary inaction.

Floorwork starts the lesson and includes:

a activities for the legs, exploring and developing the many actions possible when travelling on foot, and ways to jump and land;
b activities for the body, including the many ways to bend, stretch, rock, roll, arch, twist, curl and turn, and the many ways in which body parts receive, support and transfer the body weight in travelling and balancing;
c activities for the arms and shoulders, the least used parts of our body. We strengthen them by using them to hold all or part of the body weight, on-the-spot or moving. This strength is needed in gripping, climbing, hanging, swinging and circling, and in levering on to and across apparatus, supported by the hands only.

Apparatus work is the second part of the lesson, making varied, unique and challenging physical demands of pupils whose whole body – legs, arms and shoulders, back and abdominals – has to work strongly at more difficult:

○ travelling on hands and feet, over, under, across and around obstacles, as well as vertically, often supported only by the hands
○ jumping and landing from greater heights
○ rolling on to, along, from and across apparatus
○ gripping, swinging, climbing and circling on ropes and bars.

Final floor activity, after the apparatus has been returned to its starting places around the sides and ends of the hall, brings the whole class together again in a simple activity based on the lesson's main emphasis. After the bustle of apparatus removal – the swishing of ropes along trackways, the creaking of climbing frames being wheeled away, the bumping down of benches, planks, boxes and trestles – there is a quiet, calm, thoughtful and focused ending.

Apparatus work

Apparatus work is the most important part of the lesson and one of the most exciting areas within the programme. Pupils work, almost non-stop, at natural, popular activities as they run, jump, climb, roll, balance, swing, hang, circle and up-end, taking their weight on their hands. Three unsatisfactory systems are encountered.

1 Apparatus is never used as teachers feel insecure and fearful of accidents. Extended floorwork frustrates the pupils who thus behave badly, making the teacher even less willing to use apparatus.

2 Apparatus is brought out at the start of the morning or afternoon, and left in the same place for each class. This system, often put in place by 'apparatus monitors' (the school caretaker or welfare staff) whose apparatus lay-out applies to all classes:

   a prevents the safe teaching of floorwork and basic skills because the floor is cluttered with apparatus
   b gives no credit to the intelligence and ability of children, who enjoy and are perfectly capable of handling apparatus
   c stifles the development of any standards
   d breaches the NC requirement that pupils should be taught how to lift, carry, place and use equipment safely.

3   The apparatus is brought out from a store outside the hall, or at one end of the hall, assembled, used and then returned to the remote store, every lesson. This time-consuming system, with pile-ups at doors or at the end of the room, can take up to five minutes of the lesson time, both before and after apparatus work, instead of the minute, or less, needed in the next and recommended system.

The **recommended system** for ensuring that apparatus is lifted, carried and placed in position quickly and easily needs the co-operation of all the teachers. Before lessons start in the morning or afternoon, the portable apparatus is placed around the sides and ends of the hall adjacent to where it will be used. Each group of pupils will thus only have to carry it 2–3 metres. A well-trained class can have the apparatus in place in 30 seconds. Each day, after all lessons are finished, as much of the apparatus as possible should remain in the hall – in corners, against or on the platform, or at the sides and ends of the room. Mats can sometimes be stored vertically behind climbing frames, benches and boxes.

Organising groups for apparatus work

Because the combinations of apparatus used in infant lessons are usually simple, such as bench and mat, or low box and mat, groups of four pupils are sufficient per piece of apparatus. The organisation of the seven or eight mixed infant groups is done in September. Pupils are told, 'These are your groups and starting places for apparatus work.' For the four- or five-lesson development of a lesson, the same groups go to the same starting places, becoming more expert in lifting, carrying and placing their piece of apparatus.

   At the end of the apparatus work, groups return to their starting places to return the apparatus to its original position around the sides and ends of the room. The floor is now clear for the incoming class to start its lesson.

   For variety, and to extend their lifting and carrying expertise, groups can be placed at a new set of 'number one apparatus' at the start of the next new lesson.

Fixed and portable apparatus

Apparatus referred to in the lesson plans that follow, and shown in the examples of simple and larger apparatus groupings, include the following items:

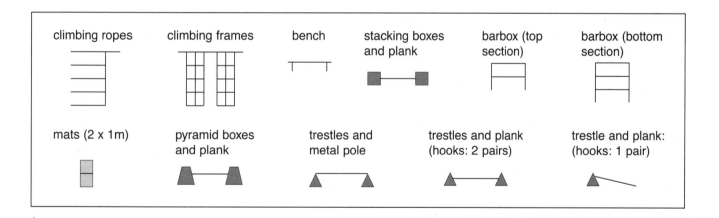

Minimum number recommended:
- 12 × mats (2 × 1 m)
- 3 × benches
- 1 × barbox that can be divided into two smaller boxes by lifting off the top section. The lower section should have a platform top
- 1 × pair stacking boxes, 19 × 19 in (48 × 48 cm) base, 13 in (33 cm) high; and one 8 ft (2.4 m) plank
- 1 × pair pyramid boxes, 31 in (78 cm) high, 24 in (60 cm) long, 21 in (53 cm) wide at base tapering to 15 in (38 cm) wide at top, and one 8 ft (2.4 m) plank
- 1 × pair of 3 ft (1 m), 3.5 ft (1.06 m), 4.6 ft (1.4 m) trestles
- 2 × planks with two pairs of hooks
- 2 × planks with one pair of hooks
- 1 × 10 ft (3 m) metal pole

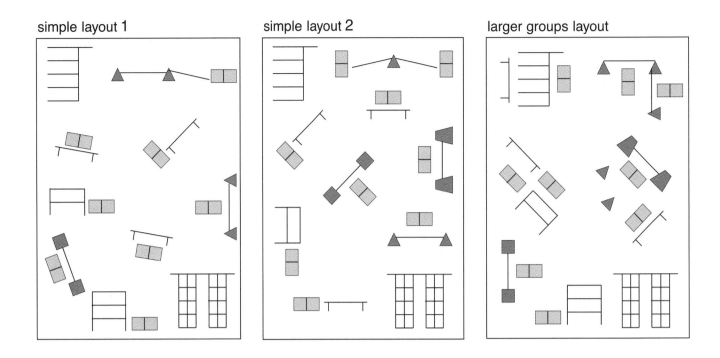

simple layout 1   simple layout 2   larger groups layout

Safe practice and accident prevention

In Physical Education lessons, where one of the main aims is to contribute to healthy growth and development, we must do everything possible to ensure safety and accident prevention.

Good supervision by the teacher at all times is a main contributor to safety. The first question asked after a serious injury is always 'Was the teacher with the class?' He or she must be there and teaching in positions from which the majority of the class can be seen. This usually means circulating on the outside looking in, with no-one behind his or her back.

Good teaching develops the correct, safe method of landing from a height; taking weight on the hands; gripping apparatus or rolling. The outward expression of the caring attitude we try to create is a sensible, unselfish sharing of hall and apparatus space, and self-control in avoiding others.

Badly behaved classes who do not respond immediately, starting or stopping as requested; who rush around selfishly and noisily, disturbing others; who are never quiet in their speech or their body movements; and who do not try to move well, are destructive of any prospect of high standards of safety or lesson enjoyment.

A safe environment requires a well-behaved, quiet, attentive and responsive class. Good behaviour must be continually pursued until it becomes the normal, expected way to work in every lesson.

The hall should be at a good working temperature, with windows and doors opened or closed as necessary, to cope with changing seasons and room temperatures. Potentially dangerous chairs, piano, tables and trolleys should be removed if possible, or pushed against a wall or into a corner. Floor sockets should be regularly cleared of cleaning substances, which harden and block the small sockets.

Before the lesson starts the teacher should check for sensible, safe clothing with no watches, rings or jewellery, which can cause serious scarring and injury, as well as long trousers that can catch heels and unbunched hair that can impede vision.

Barefoot work is recommended because it is quiet, provides a safe, strong grip on apparatus, and enhances the appearance of the work. Barefoot work also enables the little-used muscles of the feet and ankles to develop as they grip, balance, support, propel and receive the body weight.

National Curriculum requirements for Gymnastic Activities – Key Stage 1: The Main Features

'The government believes that two hours of physical activity a week, including the National Curriculum for Physical Education and extra-curricular activities, should be an aspiration for all schools. This applies to all stages.'

Programme of study

Pupils should be taught to:

a   perform basic skills in travelling; being still; finding and using space both on the floor and using apparatus
b   develop the range of their skills and actions (for example, balancing, jumping and landing, climbing, rolling)
c   link skills and actions in short movement phrases
d   create and perform short, linked sequences that show a clear beginning, middle and end with contrasts in direction, level and speed.

Attainment target

Pupils should be able to demonstrate that they can:

a   select and use skills, actions and ideas appropriately, applying them with control and co-ordination
b   copy, explore and remember skills, and link them in ways that suit the activities
c   observe and talk about differences between their own and others' performances and use this understanding to improve their own performance.

Main NC headings when considering assessment of progression and expectation

Planning thoughtfully precedes the performance. Pupils think ahead to what their response will be, trying to 'see' the intended outcome. Evidence of satisfactory planning is seen in:

a   sensible, safe judgements
b   an obvious understanding of what was asked for
c   good use of the movement elements that enhance and provide quality, variety and contrast.

Performing and improving performance is the main aim and evident as pupils:

a   work hard, concentrating on the main features of the task
b   practise to show safe, skilful, controlled activity
c   demonstrate that they can remember and repeat the actions.

Linking actions together, with control, into 'sentences of movement' with a still start and finish and a flowing middle, provides a basis for progression, and is evident as pupils:

a   work harder for longer
b   work more confidently
c   show greater use of the space, shape and effort elements that provide attractive variety and contrast in sequences.

Reflecting and making judgements is evident as pupils:

a   describe the most important features of a demonstration
b   suggest ways to improve
c   self-evaluate and act upon their own reflections.

Year 1 Gymnastic Activities programme

Pupils should be able to:

Autumn	Spring	Summer
1 Respond quietly and quickly to instructions, working continuously until stopped. **2** Co-operate unselfishly, sharing floor and apparatus space, for safe, free, unhindered movement. **3** Travel with neat, well-planned and varied use of feet on floor and on apparatus. **4** Travel, using hands and feet, with varied actions and directions, on floor and on apparatus. **5** Be body-shape aware, in balanced stillness and in travelling, with good posture and body tension. **6** Roll smoothly from side to side; rock forwards and back, and forwards roll, when ready. **7** Lift, carry, place apparatus safely with others. **8** Produce almost non-stop, neat, quiet, thoughtful activity in floor and apparatus work. **9** Travel up to, on, along and from apparatus with a good repertoire of travelling and climbing actions. **10** Absorb shock when jumping and landing from apparatus. **11** Express pleasure in demonstrations by others, and pick out and praise pleasing features.	**1** Listen, then respond to instructions, thinking about own performance. **2** Be habitually active, striving to improve. **3** Show a caring attitude to self and others. **4** Understand and use safe methods of supporting all body weight on hands – straight arms, head looking forwards. **5** Be space-aware, performing in own space, and moving from space to space. **6** Balance well on a variety of body parts, with good tension and firm shapes. **7** Jump and land safely, with no jarring, often with a direction change, from low apparatus. **8** Demonstrate an expanding repertoire of neat, well-controlled, varied movements. **9** Plan and perform sequences of simple, linked actions with still start and finish. **10** Work enthusiastically with increasing self-confidence. **11** Show pleasure from taking part in varied, vigorous, enjoyable activity. **12** Describe what was observed using simple terms to identify the movements.	**1** Respond immediately to each task set, showing a keen attitude and consideration of others sharing the space. **2** Experiment with varied actions, using opportunities given to repeat, practise and improve control and 'correctness'. **3** Practise, vary and enhance the basic actions of running, jumping, rolling, swinging, hanging, climbing, balancing and inverting. **4** Be body-shape aware, able to show firm, clear, stretched, wide, curled, arched shapes in stillness, balance and movement. **5** Be body-parts aware, understanding how parts receive, support and transfer body weight. **6** Be space aware, using different directions and levels, own and whole-room space, for variety, contrast and greater interest. **7** Land well from apparatus with a 'squashy give' in knees and ankles. **8** Use swinging as an aid and impetus to movement. **9** Demonstrate varied ways to travel up to, on, along and from apparatus, emphasising 'No queues. Use floor as well as apparatus. Be found working, not waiting.' **10** Demonstrate sequences enthusiastically, working hard to perform well to help spectators. **11** Link together a short series of actions and practise to improve and remember them. **12** Work co-operatively with a partner, leading, following, working in unison. **13** Observe others' actions and answer questions on what was seen and liked, and what was worth learning or copying.

Lesson Plan 1 • 30 minutes
September

Emphasis on: *(a) the unselfish sharing of space with a concern for own and others' safety, and immediate responses to instructions; (b) neat, well-planned use of feet and hands in travelling on floor and apparatus; (c) lifting, carrying, placing and using apparatus quietly, carefully and safely, in co-operation with others.*

Floorwork
12 minutes

Legs

1 Walk quietly in and out of one another, visiting every part of the room. Don't follow anyone.

2 Now show me your best running, moving along straight lines, not curving around, all following one another. Go to the corners, ends and sides as well as the middle.

3 Plan to show me some other way or ways you can travel, using your feet. (For example, skip, hop, bounce, gallop, slip, jump.)

Body

1 Run a few steps into a space near you, jump up high, and then do a soft, squashy landing. Spring up, look for a new space, and off you go again.

2 If you land with your feet a little bit apart, it is easier to balance still in your squashy, bent legs position.

3 Stretch arms above head in the jump, and forwards or sideways to balance you on landing. See which helps you better.

Arms

1 As you travel about slowly, using hands and feet only, can you make different parts of your body go first?

2 Try leading with head, feet, or one side of your body.

3 Can you plan some actions where only your hands travel, then only your feet?

Apparatus Work
16 minutes

1 Travel to all parts of the room without touching any apparatus. Use your feet only, and show me how you can go in and out of, along, across or under the apparatus, touching mats only.

2 Look for quiet places where you have lots of room. You can step or jump over benches, weave in and out of ropes, walk astride or along benches, jump across parts of the mats, or squeeze through spaces in the climbing frames.

3 When I call 'Stop!' find a space on the nearest apparatus and show me a fully stretched body. Now jump down quietly, and off you go again, travelling and listening for my next signal.

4 Using feet only, show me how you can travel up to, on to, along and down from the apparatus. Remember, feet only, and show me lots of good travelling on the floor as well as on apparatus.

5 Use your hands and feet to travel on the floor, up to, on to, along and down from the apparatus. Once again, you can use a jump and a squashy landing.

6 Plan to visit many different pieces of apparatus. 'Feel' the different ways that your hands and feet can support you. (You can hang, swing, crawl, circle, climb, roll, slide.)

Final Floor Activity
2 minutes

Walk, run, jump, skip and bounce in and out of one another. Visit all parts of the room.

Teaching notes and NC guidance
Development over 4 lessons

Floorwork

Legs

1   Right from the start of the year we have to work against the almost habitual anti-clockwise travelling of primary school pupils, all following one another as they curve around the outside of the room.

2   Challenge them to visit ends, sides, corners and centre, going there along a straight line and changing direction as soon as they find themselves following another.

3   Teacher commentary on the varied actions helps to expand the class repertoire. Quick demonstrations provide pictures that are remembered, copied and tried.

Body

1   The whole body is working strongly in the fully stretched position while in the air. From the upwards stretch in both arms down to the stretched ankles, the whole body should feel firm.

2   Feet can be slightly apart, side by side or one in front of the other. The squashy 'giving' landing contrasts with the firm spring upwards.

3   Pupils experiment to see whether arms stretched forwards or sideways help them balance better in the landings.

Arms

1   'Different parts going first' stops pupils all crawling forwards with bent arms and legs – the usual first response and often done far too quickly to have any physical benefits.

2   Show good examples of actions with different parts leading, and emphasise 'slow movements using the whole body strongly; straight arms for a safe, strong support; clear body shapes to add to the appearance of the performance.'

3   From a crouch position, hands and feet close together, move hands only forwards until body is fully stretched; then feet travel, either walking forwards or with a jump in. Hands and feet can be close together or wide apart, which is harder.

Apparatus Work

1   Occasionally, stop the travelling to check that all are moving, well spaced apart, never following one another and in a variety of relationships to the apparatus.

2   Teacher commentary on interesting ways to negotiate apparatus helps to inspire variety.

3   'Stop!' is an exercise in 'immediate responses to instructions', and must be answered straight away. Poor responses waste time as all wait for the casual responder to decide when to co-operate.

4   Neat, quiet travelling on the floor between apparatus should be praised and demonstrated. Point out interesting actions and uses of feet and legs. On to and from the apparatus will be a short travel, mostly walking, jumping, tiptoeing or bouncing.

5   This favourite part of the lesson, when all can go anywhere on the apparatus, is exciting, challenging and good fun. Hands and feet must both be used in travelling freely on all pieces. Look out for and comment on the varied activities going on to help the less inventive with new ideas.

6   We want pupils to experience and understand how their bodies are working, and to feel relaxed and better after vigorous activity.

Final Floor Activity

Challenge them: 'Can you join three of your favourite activities together?'

Lesson Plan 2 • 30 minutes
October

Emphasis on: *(a) whole-hearted, vigorous activity to inspire enjoyment, achievement and a sense of well-being and calm; (b) variety in travelling on feet, and feet and hands, including climbing and swinging; (c) co-operating sensibly with others to lift, carry, place and use apparatus.*

Floorwork
12 minutes

Legs

1 Can you run a few steps and jump up high, with feet together and long straight legs?

2 Now, can you run and jump up high, showing a wide body shape like a star, with arms and legs stretched wide?

3 With a neat, tall start and finish position, can you now alternate these different jumps, using a run of only 3 metres each way?

Body

1 Stand with feet slightly apart. Swing both arms forwards to a full stretch above head. With a long, slow, bouncy action, bend knees and swing arms down behind, forwards, behind, then swing arms forwards and up above head again, with a lifting up of the body.

2 It's like a ski swing. Stretch up; bend down; bounce arms backwards, forwards, backwards; swing up tall again.

Arms

1 Can you try to travel on hands and feet, keeping them wide apart? (For example, cartwheels; bouncing along on all fours; crawling with left side moving, then right side moving; wide hands only, then wide feet only.)

2 Now, can you travel with hands and feet close together? (For example, bunny jump along; close hands, then close feet travel.)

Apparatus Work
16 minutes

1 Jog around the room without stopping, touching only the floor and the mats. Can you visit each piece of apparatus and go under, over, across, along, in and out of it, always without touching it?

2 When I call 'Stop!' can you show me a beautifully long or wide stretched, still body shape on the nearest piece of apparatus?

3 Jump down quietly and continue travelling on the floor only until my next signal. Then show me your stretched or wide shape on a new body part and a new piece of apparatus.

4 On the floor between apparatus, practise again your short run and jump with high and wide body shapes. On the apparatus, find out how many ways you can support yourself with good hands and feet actions.

5 How are your hands and feet positioned when gripping a rope or a metal pole; when rolling across a mat; when bunny jumping up and over a bench or box top; when climbing the frame; when pulling along a bench; when circling around a bar?

Final Floor Activity
2 minutes

Run a few steps into a high jump, arms stretched high above head. Land with a good, squashy, knees-bent action, arms above head. Now revise the slow ski swings; down behind, forwards, backwards and all the way up. Lower arms, and off again. Strong jumps and easy ski swings.

Teaching notes and NC guidance
Development over 4 lessons

Floorwork

Legs

1   Ask the class to stay in their own personal floor space, going backwards and forwards within it, rather than all following one another around the outside of the room, being impeded by and impeding others.

2   The timing of the arm swing to assist the jump needs lots of practice. Let the class feel the firm, strong, wide position while standing, and before running and jumping to try it in flight.

3   A shuttling, there-and-back, running-and-jumping sequence needs little space. The 'explosive' drive up comes at the take-off, with knees bending and springing and the arms pulling up, rather than from a great, long run-up.

Body

1   This rhythmic, long, slow, swinging activity can be done by mirroring the teacher to start with. Every joint alternately stretches and bends, and the arm swings lead the whole movement. Fingertips can brush the floor on the 'backwards, forwards, backwards' swings.

2   When pupils understand the movement, let them swing at their own rhythm, which they may quietly say as they perform. 'One [as they swing arms up], two, three, four [bent and bouncing] and up.'

Arms

1   Wide arms and legs are as they were in one of the jumps at the start. Straight arms are strong and safe. Emphasise this so that pupils' arms are habitually straight when inverted or on hands and feet.

2   Hands and feet close together is easier, physically, than when they are apart. It is possible to include some moments when all the weight is on the hands, as in a bunny jump forwards and on to hands only.

Apparatus Work

1   Pursue good quality movement by praising and demonstrating with pupils whose walking, running, jumping, bouncing and skipping is neat, quiet, well-controlled, never following others and appropriate for the part of the room where they are doing it.

2   Quiet feet, quiet pupils moving and listening for the teacher in a quiet voice to call 'Stop!' is a desirable tradition. This usually means a safe, well-ordered environment and few stoppages.

3   The quick reaction to the teacher's instruction is matched by the need for quick planning to decide which body part and new shape to use on the next 'Stop!' Ask for a firm, strong, hard-working body in the held shape, with no lazy sagging.

4   The runs and jumps on the floor can be adjusted to arrive on a mat, so that pupils are near a piece of apparatus to mount and travel on. Teacher commentary on actions which make good use of hands and feet support will expand the class repertoire.

5   As in the floorwork, let the hands and feet travelling be slow, careful and thoughtful. As well as the straight, safe arms when weight is mainly on hands, emphasise the 'thumbs under' grip on bars for safety.

Final Floor Activity

This sequence includes good variety with its stillness at start and finish; its run and vigorous leap with strong body shape; and its slow, easy swinging on the spot.

Lesson Plan 3 • 30 minutes
November

Emphasis on: *(a) body parts awareness as you plan and carry out tasks; (b) pursuit of near non-stop, quiet, neat, thoughtful, focused activity, both in floorwork and in travelling up to, on and from apparatus.*

Floorwork
12 minutes

Legs

1 Can you show me a variety of ways you can travel, using one foot, both feet or one foot after the other?

2 'Variety' means more than one activity, i.e. using at least two different moves, such as skipping forwards, then two-footed bouncing sideways.

3 Please travel along straight lines, never curving around or following others.

Body

1 From different starting positions can you travel by going from body part to body part? (For example, from feet to knees, to seat, to lying on back, to shoulders.)

2 How are you linking your positions together? (Lowering, sitting, rocking, twisting, stretching, rolling.)

3 Can you include a hard-working, clear body shape at each position? (No lazy sagging.)

Arms

1 Can you try a little bunny jump, keeping arms straight and knees bent?

2 Fingers point forwards and arms are straight for a strong position.

3 In a brilliant bunny jump your shoulders are above your hips, which are above your hands.

Apparatus Work
16 minutes

1 Show me your favourite ways to travel on feet on the floor only, not touching any apparatus except the mats.

2 Can you include some of the variety from your floorwork as you go under, over, across, along, or in and out of the apparatus, still without touching it? (A hop across a mat; a two-footed bounce astride a bench; walking and running often.)

3 Now move on to the apparatus, visiting pieces that are not crowded. How many parts of your body can grip the apparatus as you travel on it? (Hands and feet climb on ropes and climbing frame; back of knees and hands grip under a pole; tummy and hands circle on a bar; hands only swing on a rope; hands pull along a plank; feet take you along benches, planks, boxes.)

4 Can you arrive on the apparatus using your hands strongly to lift, twist, pull, lever, swing, roll you on? Make your feet important when you leave the apparatus.

5 Go from apparatus to apparatus, touching each piece with hands only, and show me a bunny jump with straight arms and well-bent legs.

Final Floor Activity
2 minutes

Stand with feet together and do an upwards jump. Run forwards a very short distance (about 3 metres) and into a second jump. Use your stretched arms to help you balance in the air and on landing.

Teaching notes and NC guidance
Development over 4 lessons

Floorwork

Legs

1 Planning to include examples of travelling on one, two and alternate feet is a good challenge. The teacher will need to be observant in identifying and commenting on the varied examples if the class repertoire is to be extended.

2 Ask half the class to observe the other half, and to look out for and name the actions seen, in order to share ideas. 'Variety' can be based on different actions, directions or body shapes (star jump different to tucked jump, for example).

3 Lesson after lesson, we want straight travelling in to own spaces. Too often in primary schools, all follow each other anti-clockwise in a big circle.

Body

1 With a less responsive or creative class, the teacher can lead pupils through a series of starting positions to get the activity going. We want a travel element and a still, held element that has good body tension and a neat appearance.

2 Once again, the teacher can call out and suggest the links. 'From standing tall and still, all lower down to kneeling; rock back on to your seat; lower back to lying; now swing up on to shoulders.'

3 Ask class to 'feel strong, with muscles firm'. Our bodies work harder and look neater when we make our shapes firm and clear.

Arms

1 'Show me your hands' will have whole class holding hands towards teacher, who checks that arms are straight with fingers pointing forwards: two important safety elements when inverted.

2 Pupils crouch down and place the hands on the floor, under the shoulders. Body weight is forwards on flat hands and tips of toes.

3 One or two little preparatory jumps off the floor with both feet precede the stronger push up on to hands.

Apparatus work

1 During this period, while the class is travelling freely without touching apparatus, the teacher can make last-minute adjustments to the apparatus positions. Ensure that none is too near the side or end walls and that all mats are properly placed.

2 Class are asked to plan examples of travelling on one, two and alternate feet, as already practised in the floorwork. Such travelling must be used as appropriate, as in the examples given.

3 A lesson on 'body-parts awareness' works the best, of course, when the class are challenged to support themselves, travel, climb, swing, balance and move on apparatus. In this lesson, the focus is on the body parts concerned.

4 The focus now is on how to use your hands to bring, mount, swing, pull, lever or roll yourself on to the different pieces of apparatus. Feel the different actions taking place. Safe controlled steps, jumps or bounces are the focus in leaving the apparatus and 'making the feet important'.

5 Children are sensible about how high they lift feet off the floor. The unsure do a tentative, low lift of feet and bent legs. The more confident make their bunny jumps go higher off the floor.

Final Floor Activity

Pupils should be aware of feet in run and jump; of arms in air and on landing; of whole, still body at the start and finish.

Lesson Plan 4 • 30 minutes
December

Emphasis on: *(a) body-shape awareness, in stillness and in motion; (b) improving the look of the work by making the body shape precise; (c) expressing pleasure in demonstrations by others, and picking out the main features in a demonstration.*

Floorwork
12 minutes

Legs

1 Can you run and jump up high with feet together and long, straight legs?

2 Try one- and two-footed take-offs to see which gives you the better jump upwards.

3 When you land, use long, straight arms up, forwards or sideways to help you balance.

4 Now run and jump high, showing a wide shape like a star, with arms and legs stretched wide.

Body

1 Lie on your back, curled up small, with hands clasped under knees. Can you rock backwards and forwards, keeping your body curled and head on knees?

2 Now, can you roll from side to side, still curled up small and round, with hands clasped under knees?

3 Can you roll from side to side, then to the first side, and right over on to tummy and on to back again? To one side; to other side; to first side and right over.

Arms

1 Start crouched on hands and feet, small and curled in. Travel to a long, stretched position, still on hands and feet, by moving hands or feet only. Move back to your crouch position by moving hands or feet only.

2 With straight arms and legs in the travel, your body will be working very hard. Try it.

3 Feel if it is harder to travel with straight arms and legs close together or wide apart.

Apparatus Work
16 minutes

1 Run quietly around the room, not touching any apparatus. When I call 'Stop!' show me a clear body shape on the nearest piece of apparatus. 'Stop!' Are you really stretched, wide, curled or arched?

2 Run around again. On my next signal, show me a new body shape on a different piece of apparatus. 'Stop!'

3 Travel from apparatus to apparatus, putting hands only on each piece and jumping feet up off floor, as in a bunny jump. Show me strong, straight arms and well-bent legs while on your hands.

4 Travel freely on all the apparatus, showing me different actions as you move up to, on to, along and from the apparatus.

5 In all your travelling, make your whole body shape clear and firm as you work hard to make your work look neater and better.

6 Can you leave the apparatus sometimes with a high jump and a squashy landing, then a sideways roll on the mat, curled up like a little ball?

Final Floor Activity
2 minutes

Run and jump stretched; run and jump wide; then run and jump with own choice of body shape.

Teaching notes and NC guidance
Development over 4 lessons

Floorwork

Legs

1 Because the jumping is the main activity, the run should only be for three or four strides. Discourage those who run all around the room (disturbing others) before doing their jump.

2 An upwards jump is more easily done from a two-footed take-off. Both feet are under you, driving upwards.

3 In addition to improving the appearance of the work, straight arms act like a tightrope walker's pole, helping you to balance.

4 Demonstrate with outstanding performers. Hard work is needed to achieve a wide shape in the short time the body is in flight.

Body

1 Use step-by-step teaching to put pupils in the correct, curled starting position. 'Lie down on your back. Curl up small with your back rounded. Clasp your hands together under your knees. Put your head on your knees. Swing back and rock on to your shoulders. Now, swing forwards, back on to your seat.'

2 The impetus for the sideways movement comes from the knees swinging to that side.

3 The impetus for the complete roll over comes from a strong pull to that side by the bent legs and head.

Arms

1 The class can mirror the teacher so that they are all in the low, crouched starting position, with weight equally on hands and feet. They then have to plan their move to the contrasting stretched position, travelling on hands only or feet only.

2 On straight arms and legs, our crouch position is more of an arch, demanding suppleness and strength.

3 A high arch results from hands and feet being close together. A much lower arch (very hard to support) results from hands and feet being wider apart.

Apparatus Work

1 This activity demands an immediate response to a signal, followed by quick decision-making on where to go to show a clear body shape. Praise those pupils who have found an excellent space to show an admirable, firm, clear, hard-working body shape.

2 Ideally, the new body shape will also be performed on a new supporting body part, not always on feet, which are most commonly used.

3 The bunny jump was introduced last month and is here being practised for further improvement. It helps to take off from a starting position where feet are very near to the apparatus.

4 From the 'one touch only and away' of the bunny jumps, pupils now linger and travel further on the apparatus, focusing first of all on the actions being performed. They should be thinking 'I am climbing, swinging, balancing, rolling, jumping, stepping, sliding, pulling, hanging, circling, lowering.'

5 Their focus now should be on body shapes that are neat, correct, safe and attractive as they travel through the actions above.

6 We have practised high jumps, squashy landings and sideways rolls, and are now trying to link them together smoothly.

Final Floor Activity

Two-thirds of the activity are teacher-led. The pupils have to plan what their third activity will be. The whole sequence can be done around a small triangle.

Lesson Plan 5 ● 30 minutes
January

Emphasis on: *(a) space awareness and the unselfish sharing of space with a concern for own and others' safety; (b) linking actions in a well-planned way, and demonstrating enthusiastically when asked.*

Floorwork
12 minutes

Legs

1 Can you travel around the room using your feet, sometimes facing forwards and sometimes in another direction?

2 You can try walking forwards, bouncing sideways, and, very carefully, skipping backwards.

3 Are you looking for quiet parts of the room to go in to each time?

Body

1 Can you show me a still balance with part of your body stretched up to a high level?

2 Now change to being on a different body part, with another part stretched high. (For example, from standing on tiptoes with one arm upstretched; to being on one foot and two hands with one leg upstretched; to being on seat with legs and arms upstretched.)

3 Can you be very clever and join up two or three balances and stretches?

Arms

1 Can you take your weight on your hands, lift your legs up in to the air, then bring them down quietly in a new place?

2 Pretend that the floor is a bench and you are taking your feet from one side to the other, while on your hands. You can try this later on the benches.

3 Remember to keep your arms straight for a strong position, and your head looking forwards (not back under the arms, which makes everything appear upside-down).

Apparatus Work
16 minutes

1 As you travel on the floor and mats only, not touching any apparatus yet, can you visit every part of the room – the ends, sides, corners and middle?

2 You may go under, across, along and in and out of the apparatus, but still no touching. Keep moving and looking for the quiet spaces where you will have lots of room.

3 Use the floor and the apparatus to show me travelling where you are near to the apparatus. (For example, tight grip on ropes and climbing frames; pulling, sliding low along benches and planks; circling on metal poles and climbing-frame bars; rolls on mats.)

4 On feet only, travel up to and on to the apparatus. Show me a high stretched balance above the apparatus. Then do an upwards jump off, followed by a squashy landing and a sideways roll on a mat.

5 Can you arrive on and leave the apparatus at different places and in different ways?

Final Floor Activity
2 minutes

Run and jump to land facing a new direction.

Teaching notes and NC guidance
Development over 4 lessons

Floorwork

Legs

1 Demonstrate the meanings of 'forwards, backwards, sideways' with a follow-the-leader start, all copying the teacher. Within that practice, ask for special care on the backwards movements, which should not last long for safety's sake.

2 Demonstrations of varied ways to travel will quickly increase the class repertoire, as will suggestions by the teacher (who is, after all, teaching, as well as encouraging originality and drawing out ideas).

3 Sometimes a 'quiet part' is the space where you are already. Stay there for a second or two if the floor ahead is busy. All the actions normally done on the move can also be done on-the-spot.

Body

1 Define a 'balance' as 'when your body is held still on some small or unusual part, not wobbling because you are working hard to hold it steady'.

2 While the stretched part is always extending high, the idea of working at different levels can be put across here. Each balance can be shown at a different level, i.e. high, medium or low.

3 The whole sequence is done slowly, showing clearly the linking movements such as bending down; lowering to sitting; twisting on to a different part; rolling up on to shoulders.

Arms

1 The idea of 'air space' in addition to floor space is being explained and put across here. Many of our gymnastic activities happen in the space above and around us. Much of the work also happens on our hands, which are often working as hard as our feet and legs, particularly on apparatus.

2 'Let's pretend...' helps to give a picture of the desired pattern.

3 It is a good idea to ask pupils to hold the crouched, ready position for the teacher to check; straight arms; head looking forwards; fingers pointing forwards.

Apparatus Work

1 Challenge the class to visit all parts of the room, weaving in and out of all the apparatus and sharing the space sensibly with others.

2 The 'under, over, along, across, in and out of, through' inspires lots of interesting activities and a first-hand experience of the meaning of these prepositions.

3 Class should use a variety of ways to hold on to (with arms and legs) and travel along (on, under, around or across) apparatus, in close proximity to each piece.

4 In 'feet only' travelling, the ropes are out of bounds because you need both hands and feet on a rope. The majority of infant school apparatus is low (mats, benches, planks, parts of boxes) so that this task is easily worked at, with plenty of pieces for all to share. The 'travel; balance; jump; land; roll' is a good example of linking actions into gymnastic sequences.

5 There is a dual challenge to plan for, namely to arrive on and leave the apparatus at different places, and to demonstrate different actions when mounting and leaving it.

Final Floor Activity

'Can you run and jump four times, and land facing a different side of the room each time?'

Lesson Plan 6 • 30 minutes
February

Emphasis on: *(a) jumping and landing, learning to absorb shock; (b) rolling; (c) repeating, practising, improving and remembering sequences of linked actions.*

Floorwork
12 minutes

Legs

1   Jump and land in your own floor space. Spring up with a good stretch in your ankles. Land softly and quietly by letting your ankles, knees and hips 'give' like springs.

2   Use a short run, then jump up high from one or both feet. Feel your nice, squashy landing, with knees bending well.

3   Let's join them together now. Do one jump on the spot, then do a very short run in to a second upwards jump. Aim for a silent landing each time.

Body

1   Lie on your back, curled up small, and roll backwards and forwards from your seat all the way to your shoulders.

2   With your hands beside your shoulders, thumbs in, fingers out, push the floor while on your shoulders, to rock you back to sitting.

3   With hands clasped under knees, still curled up on your back, can you roll smoothly from side to side?

4   Lie on your back with your body straight. Can you twist to one side to roll over on to your front, then over on to your back again?

Arms

1   Can you join together two or three bunny jumps on-the-spot with some travelling using hands and feet?

2   Do all the movements slowly so that I can see clearly what your interesting actions are.

3   Try to remember your actions exactly. (For example, hands only to walk forwards for 6 counts, then feet to bounce forwards for 4 counts.)

Apparatus Work
16 minutes

1   As you travel all around the room, without touching any apparatus, can you include safe jumps across parts of mats, over benches and low planks?

2   Working nearer the apparatus now, can you show me jumping movements, still without touching any apparatus? (For example, bouncing, feet astride and along benches or planks; jumping, feet together; weaving in and out of ropes; jumping from a standing start across a low barbox with a good arm swing to help you.)

3   Jump and land on a mat, do a soft, squashy landing, then a sideways roll to bring you on to hands and feet. Jump up, and off you go again.

4   Travel freely on floor and apparatus now. In your travelling, I would like to see your movements done slowly and clearly. With a nicely stretched body, can you jump up and off the apparatus, land softly and lower into a smooth, sideways roll?

5   You may add in rolling on mats and rolling from apparatus. For example, rolling from sitting, kneeling, lying on benches, planks or low box tops. You choose. Roll forwards or sideways.

Final Floor Activity
2 minutes

Show me how softly and silently you can do four jumps to each side of the room in turn.

Teaching notes and NC guidance
Development over 4 lessons

Floorwork

Legs

1 Ankles are seldom stretched fully in everyday life, so many will be stiff. A demonstration by someone with strong, supple ankles is essential to show how to stretch beautifully on take-off and 'give' on landing.

2 The short run will be of three or four strides only. Once again, we want to feel the ankles stretching as the driving force at take-off. A squashy landing is felt as the knees give.

3 Sequences of linked actions can be as simple as this jump on the spot; then the run and jump; then the landing; plus, of course the still, upright, proud starting and finishing positions.

Body

1 When rolling, it helps to think of a body part that swings you in to the rolls. From being curled up on your back, the legs swing you forwards, and the upper body swings you backwards.

2 The hands at shoulders position lets you practise the equivalent of the start of a backward roll from sitting, and the end of a forward roll from being on shoulders.

3 Together, the knees and clasped hands swing you from side to side. Elbows in and head on chest keep you nicely rounded.

4 A twist to roll to the right is started by the left leg or the left shoulder coming across. Some pupils dislike rolling on a rounded back, but don't mind doing it with a straight body.

Arms

1 One lesson emphasis is the 'practising, improving and remembering' of sequences and linked movements. Two or three different actions and the associated one or two linking movements have to be planned and remembered to allow repetition.

2 'No quick scampering!' so that full, clear actions are being performed at a speed that calls for good strength and control.

3 The teacher can say 'Pretend I am watching each one of you to see exactly what you are doing. Repeat your sequence, time after time, to help me.'

Apparatus Work

1 The run and jump practices of the start of the lesson are now being practised to clear low apparatus carefully and only when you have a good space to land on.

2 Instead of approaching, clearing and moving away from apparatus, we now stay near it, still practising jumping as we travel next to, along or in and out of it.

3 There will be nine or ten mats widely spaced about the room. We are now linking a run, jump, landing and a sideways roll, to be followed by a lively spring up on to both feet. Run away again, looking for the next clear mat.

4 The mixture of travelling freely on all apparatus, particularly using hands and feet; jumping off with a nicely stretched body; landing softly, knees 'giving'; then rolling sideways, makes an attractive sequence of varied and contrasting activities.

5 Rolls can start from on a piece of apparatus, in addition to the obvious starts from the side of a mat.

Final Floor Activity

Class activities where all work in unison are popular. This one has everybody starting facing the front and working around to each side, four by four.

Lesson Plan 7 • 30 minutes
March

Emphasis on: *(a) balance held with good body tension and a good body shape; (b) increasing self-confidence showing through in positive effort; (c) pleasure evident in enthusiastic participation.*

Floorwork
12 minutes

Legs

1   Stand tall and still. Now lift one foot off the floor and hold your balance by leaning to one side a little bit. Change feet and balance again.

2   Travel about the hall on your feet in many ways. When I call 'Stop!' be perfectly balanced, still and on tiptoes.

3   Now change to running a few steps, then jumping and landing in a beautifully balanced position, where your body is working hard to avoid wobbling. A stretching of both arms sideways or forwards will help your balance.

Body

1   Can you make up a sequence of three stretched body shapes that are also balances because they are difficult to hold still? Move from one to the next, stretching and being still again.

2   'Balance' means being on small or unusual body parts. Are you planning to be on small as well as unusual parts? (For example, on one foot; tiptoes; seat; shoulders; elbows and knees; one hand and one foot; one knee and one hand; two hands.)

3   The balance will look neater and your body will be working harder if your stretches are really strong and firm.

Arms

1   Crouch down on hands and feet, with weight forwards on your hands. Try two little bounces, lifting your feet off the floor a little way. Then, on three, push off strongly with both feet up to a good bunny-jump position. Can you hold the balance on your hands for two or three counts?

2   Keep both arms straight, hands pointing forwards and head looking forwards to help your position and your balance.

3   If you want to try a handstand balance, do it with your swinging-up leg going well forwards, and the kicking leg staying back.

Apparatus Work
16 minutes

1   There are many low pieces of apparatus spaced around the hall. Travel up to a piece and jump over it to land and hold a balance for a second or two before moving on to a new piece.

2   Spacing out well, run around, using the floor only. When I call 'Stop!' show me a still, firm balance on the nearest piece of apparatus.

3   When I stop you next time, show me a balance on a different body part on a new piece of apparatus. Can we have less balancing on feet only? 'Stop!'

4   From a still starting position away from apparatus, travel up to and on to a piece of apparatus, and show me a still, beautifully stretched balance for two or three counts. Then leave the apparatus to finish in a neat, still position. Repeat up to and on to a new piece.

5   Spend more time now staying and travelling on pieces of apparatus. Within your travelling please let me see how often you can be in a strong, firm balance on different body parts.

Final Floor Activity
2 minutes

Balance, standing on one foot, body steady. Now change to the other foot and hold body steady but in a different position to the first balance.

Teaching notes and NC guidance
Development over 4 lessons

Floorwork

Legs

1   This simple balance can help the class to feel how hard their bodies work to remain still when balanced on a smaller part than usual. Arms will stretch sideways and the body will lean to the opposite side almost automatically to help keep balance.

2   If pupils stop, standing on two feet as normal, no balance is involved. Emphasise the 'stretched, still balance on tiptoes' to make it a challenging balance.

3   Once again, the still position at the end of the landing has to be on the balls of the feet to make it a balance. The feet can be apart, one in front of the other or side by side; or they can be together, which is a difficult balance.

Body

1   Introduce this activity with the challenge 'Show me a beautifully stretched balance position, standing on tiptoes. Now lift one foot off the floor and balance on the other foot, still showing me an excellent, stretched, whole body shape.' Then ask class to start finding other body parts to hold a still, stretched balance on.

2   As well as the standing start positions suggested by the teacher, the class can think about having front, back or side towards the floor, or being up-ended, as on shoulders. (Half of class watching and commenting on the supporting parts used by the other half demonstrating will add to class repertoire.)

3   Say 'In your balance, let your body sag and be lazy. Now, let's do it properly and firm up the whole body. Really stretch the parts not being used to support you. Feel the difference.'

Arms

1   Practice gets pupils to feel how much effort to put into a push from feet on to hands. Bent legs lift up quite easily.

2   Demonstrate with good performers to explain 'Arms straight and head looking forwards' for a strong, safe, compact position.

3   In the handstand, the one leg far forwards and one leg back almost make a straight line. This helps the balance like the long pole of the tightrope walker.

Apparatus Work

1   This is like the third activity of the floorwork with a low obstacle to force a high jump. We want a balanced landing, ideally on the balls of the feet, with arms stretched firmly.

2   Do not allow wandering to balance on a favourite piece. They must go straight to the nearest, and plan and decide quickly how and where to balance.

3   Unless taught otherwise, the majority will simply stand semi-balanced on their feet. We want them to try holding a firm, nicely stretched balance on lower legs, seat, shoulders, one hand and one foot (front, back or side to floor), tummy, elbow and hand.

4   A starting position; travel; mounting and balancing on apparatus; dismounting; and going to a finish position on the floor, all add up to an interesting and varied sequence of seven parts.

5   Travelling on a variety of supporting parts alternates with balancing on a variety of parts. This provides variety and contrast, two important features of good sequences.

Final Floor Activity

The upper body can lean to one side or horizontally forwards, or be arched backwards.

Lesson Plan 8 • 30 minutes
April

Emphasis on: *(a) working harder for longer, linking two or more simple actions to plan and create sequences; (b) demonstrating an expanding repertoire of well-controlled, neat body movements.*

Floorwork
12 minutes

Legs

1 Using a still start and finish each time, can you show me a short sequence of favourite ways to travel using feet only?

2 Can you name the two or three different actions you are including and remembering?

3 Can you include varied actions (not always running and jumping) performed in a variety of ways (e.g. using different directions, shapes, speeds)?

Body

1 Try to join together two or three arched, bridge-like shapes.

2 This shape will have three or four sides, one of which is usually the floor.

3 Please try a high bridge, like standing with your upper body reaching down. Then try bridges at a medium level (e.g. crab arch) and a low level (e.g. lying on your back with an arch between shoulders and heels).

Arms

1 Plan to show me an interesting pathway as you travel using both hands and feet.

2 You can go forwards and backwards to the same place; or around three sides of a triangle; or, if you are feeling strong and full of ideas, around four sides of a square.

3 The variety and contrast, which is pleasing to see, can come from a change of direction, body shape or level (e.g. high cartwheels and low travel on hands and feet).

Apparatus Work
16 minutes

1 Stand on the floor, perfectly still. Travel up to your nearest piece of apparatus using feet only; travel on to and along the apparatus, using both hands and feet; somewhere show me a bridge-like shape on your apparatus; leave the apparatus and return to a still finish position on the floor. Practise this sequence several times at the same piece of apparatus, so that you can remember and improve it.

2 I would like to see a jump and a squashy landing somewhere. This could be on to a mat before you go on to the other apparatus, or it could be our way of leaving the apparatus. You might even include a sideways roll after the landing.

3 All move to a new piece of apparatus and stand still, ready to start again. Remember to show me your best still start and finish positions, as well as your travelling; your making a bridge; and your jumping and landing. Stay at your present apparatus to practise, improve and remember your sequence.

4 As well as the neat, still start and finish positions, I am looking for neat, quiet, well-controlled actions; good, clear body shapes; and a change of direction or level somewhere for variety and contrast.

Final Floor Activity
2 minutes

Using feet only, show me a still, well-stretched balance. Travel a few steps into a different balance. Travel to a third, different balance.

Teaching notes and NC guidance
Development over 4 lessons

Floorwork

Legs

1 'Short' means two or three, so that the whole sequence is short enough to be remembered, but long enough to be interesting to perform.

2 Re-inforce the thoughtful planning by asking some of the class to name their actions, then demonstrate them.

3 Varied actions could be hopping on one foot; bouncing on both feet; and jumping from one to both feet.

Body

1 If the class are asked to point out some examples of bridge-like shapes in the room, they will more clearly understand the kind of shape that is wanted.

2 If responses are slow, the teacher can lead the class through a bridge on two feet, with upper body bent forwards and down; then a bridge on one hand and one foot, side towards the floor; then seated with the 'bridge' under both knees.

3 The high arch on feet can be to the front, rear or either side. If a crab is too hard, pupils can have their front towards the floor, on hands and feet.

Arms

1 Depending on the space available and whether pupils wish to practise two or more different actions, they will work on a straight line or a larger figure.

2 'A different action for each part of your two-, three- or four-sided figure, done slowly and in control' is the challenge.

3 Decide on the actions first, making the body parts work neatly, in good control. Next, make the shapes firm and clear, particularly any stretches that work the body strongly. A change of direction to the side or zig-zagging, and/or a change of level, are always signs of thoughtful, versatile work.

Apparatus Work

1 Pupils can stay at the apparatus they brought out as an easy way to ensure equal numbers everywhere. Their forward planning is being called on to work out: (a) their pathway from the starting position on floor to apparatus, and to finishing position on floor; (b) how and where they will travel throughout; (c) where it is appropriate to include the still, bridge-like shape.

2 Still at the same apparatus, now add the jump and landing, and the opportunity to include a roll. To ensure that the work is focused and thoughtful, pupils might be forewarned 'In a minute or two I will ask for volunteers to demonstrate the sequences you have been practising, improving and remembering.'

3 On alternate weeks pupils can move clockwise and anti-clockwise to the next piece of apparatus. Ensure variety by aiming to visit three pieces each lesson. By organising groups to demonstrate the sharing of floor and apparatus space, and their near non-stop work, we show examples of what can be achieved at apparatus places still to be visited.

4 Ample praise should be given for good effort at this difficult and challenging level of work being asked for.

Final Floor Activity

An A... B... C... pattern sequence with each of the three parts different and taking very little space.

Lesson Plan 9 • 30 minutes
May

Emphasis on: *(a) partner work as a valuable contribution to learning to work co-operatively; (b) developing the ability to observe and recognise another's actions; (c) making appreciative comments and judgements on another's performance.*

Floorwork
12 minutes

Legs

1   In pairs, follow your leader around the room, travelling on feet only. Keep about 2 metres behind your partner so that you can see the foot and leg actions clearly.

2   Leader, can you do more than one action for your partner to see and copy?

3   Can you travel almost mirroring each other's actions, shapes and directions?

Body

1   Show each other a favourite balance where part of your body is stretched strongly.

2   Can you do these two balances slowly and carefully, one after the other, working together?

3   Is it possible to make a gentle contact, with the stretched body parts touching each time?

Arms

1   Let's have a new leader this time. (Follower at start of leg activity.) Take your partner travelling on hands and feet, with two or three interesting, favourite actions.

2   Lead very slowly, maybe travelling a short distance, then waiting for your partner to observe and catch up.

3   For variety, try changing direction or letting a different body part lead.

Apparatus Work
16 minutes

1   Follow your leader up to, over, across, along, under, or in and out of apparatus, without touching anything other than mats. Keep about 2 metres apart, going along non-stop; or leader goes ahead and stops while partner watches, then catches up.

2   With great care, new leader, show your partner a run and jump to bring you on to a mat, or to take you over a piece of very low apparatus.

3   Now the leader will show you how to arrive on a piece of apparatus using hands only, and how to leave carefully using feet only. Take your time and wait until you have plenty of space, particularly if you are jumping off, landing and then rolling.

4   Start in a floor space at opposite sides of your piece of apparatus, and about 3 or 4 metres away from it. Together, travel up to and on to the apparatus, pass each other carefully, and finish in your partner's starting place.

Final Floor Activity
2 minutes

Stand facing each other. With a little bending of the knees as a starting signal, can you bounce on the spot at exactly the same speed, mirroring each other?

Teaching notes and NC guidance
Development over 4 lessons

Floorwork

Legs

1   Emphasise that a good leader looks after the following partner by keeping his or her eyes open for good spaces to travel through, and by staying on straight lines, not curving around following everyone else. By stopping the class often to check that pairs are reasonably together and well spaced, the teacher can comment positively on good examples of leadership for others to observe and copy.

2   Two or three different actions continually being repeated makes an interesting sequence if the couples are together.

3   You watch your partner's actions first. Then you watch the shapes that are firm and clear. Then you hope for a change of direction at some point to add variety to the performance.

Body

1   One watches while the other performs. Then they change duties. The observer looks to see which body parts are supporting and which are strongly stretched to enhance the appearance.

2   After several practices, pupils move on to performing the two balances one after the other, both finishing in the held position.

3   In the held position, they now make a gentle contact between the body parts stretching. They need to plan their starting relationship to ensure that a contact happens easily.

Arms

1   Well spaced out to start with, couples should remain in their own parts of the room, working around a triangle or square shape.

2   Travel; stop. Partner following ensures that the leader thinks about the actions, and leader ensures that the follower watches to copy. This is better than silly scampering, chasing one after the other.

3   Variety in actions might be difficult to plan, but the variety inherent in changing direction and leading parts will help.

Apparatus Work

1   They will prefer following non-stop, therefore the leader must go slowly and never become mixed up with other couples. Remind the leaders 'If it suddenly becomes crowded, stop your travelling, and your following partner should stop with you'.

2   Sometimes waiting before the run and the jump will be essential to avoid bumps and accidents, as all share the nine or ten mats in a typical layout.

3   Follower stands and watches partner's method of mounting the apparatus, making the hands important. While follower comes on to apparatus, the leader waits. Leader leaves the apparatus, making feet important, while follower observes. Follower comes from apparatus and they finish at a place from which they start again, either at the same apparatus, or towards another piece.

4   Coming towards the sides of a plank, bench, box or climbing frame, there will be plenty of room to pass each other, side by side. If they are coming along the length of a bench, plank, pole or on the same trestle, one should pause while the other tries to negotiate the still partner.

Final Floor Activity

The 'one, two, three, four' count of pupils' feet on the floor should be felt, leading them at just the right speed.

Lesson Plan 10 • 30 minutes
June

Emphasis on: *(a) swinging as an aid and impetus to movement; (b) making the hall a 'scene of busy activity', inspired by an enthusiastic attitude to participation.*

Floorwork
12 minutes

Legs

1 Stand with your knees slightly bent and both arms stretched behind you. Can you swing your arms forwards and up to help an upwards jump on the spot?

2 Do three of these jumps, all facing the same way, without stopping, letting your arms swing well backwards and forwards each time. Feel how your arms seem to pull you up.

3 Stand with your knees slightly bent and one arm raised to one side at about hip height. Can you swing this arm into a jump to face the next side of the room? Do this four times back to your starting place, then try it around the other way, using the other arm to swing you.

Body

1 Lie on your back, curled up small with your hands clasped under your knees. Your chin is on your chest so that you are curled from seat to head. Swing from side to side into sideways rolls, and feel which part your body is helping by its swinging action.

2 Sit, curled up again. This time your hands are next to your shoulders. Rock back on to your hands, then push forwards on to your seat again. Can you feel how your head, then your feet help the movement by swinging you backwards and forwards?

3 Lie stretched out on your back, hands by your sides. To help you to roll on to your front, swing with the opposite leg or shoulder, or both together.

Arms

1 Can you swing up on to your hands? Try a swing of both arms from a start above your head, keeping them straight.

2 Try to swing the kicking leg up behind you. Remember to keep looking forwards so that everything looks normal, not upside-down, as it does if you look back under the arms.

3 You choose now. Use the swinging method you found the best, and practise your handstands carefully.

Apparatus Work
16 minutes

1 Can you do a short run and swing into an upwards jump on to a mat or any of the low apparatus? You should feel the swing coming from an arm or a leg. You can swing up and from the apparatus, using both arms as we did at the very start of the lesson.

2 Continue with this practice, but you may now add in a roll on a mat with a curled or a stretched body that swings to one side. Then you jump up, and off you go again.

3 Now visit low pieces of apparatus, including mats, and put your hands on each piece with fingers pointing forwards and arms straight. Can you swing one leg up behind you to put all your weight on your hands for a second or two?

4 Practise freely on all the apparatus and try to include: (a) a swing on to and from apparatus; (b) a swing into a roll; (c) a swing up to take all the weight on your hands.

Final Floor Activity
2 minutes

Follow your leader's travelling and swinging into a jump.

Teaching notes and NC guidance
Development over 4 lessons

Floorwork

Legs

1   A demonstration by the teacher of the starting hands and knees positions and the lively upwards swing will get the lesson off to a busy start.

2   The stretched arms should feel strong at the end of the swing and be working as hard as the legs to give the whole body an attractive, well-controlled look. The gentle 'give' in the knees and ankles on landing should be asked for and demonstrated.

3   Left arm swings to right to make a quarter turn that is easily controlled, even when coming off apparatus later.

Body

1   A really good, swinging, sideways roll can take you right over on to your front, then on to your back again.

2   This practice gives a feel for the start of a backward roll and the end of a forward roll.

3   Many pupils do not like rolling on a curled back, but do not mind rolling with a straight body. The swinging pull of the parts that start the action is very obvious when the body is straight.

Arms

1   This long lever swing, with both arms starting above the head, is very strong and liable to make pupils overswing. Some like it.

2   This lesser lever swing of the foot kicking up behind is easier to control and the hands are down near the floor to start with.

3   Let pupils decide. The one they choose will be the one they use for practice from now on. Both methods have their supporters.

Apparatus Work

1   There are lots of low surfaces, including mats, to share and work on. The little run adds to the force of the eventual swing. They are now thinking of, focusing on and planning to use swings to aid their jumps on to and from the various apparatus.

2   Ideally, the sideways roll will come after a squashy landing from the jump up and off apparatus. It should form part of the landing, expanding pupils' work by giving it variety and contrast.

3   This is halfway between a bunny jump and a handstand. Hands start on the apparatus, but only one leg does the swinging up behind action. If pupils wish to twist to come down on a new floor space, there will be a little swing to that side by the legs and hips.

4   The combination of mounting, travelling along and leaving apparatus, including a roll and weight on hands at some point, makes this a nicely varied sequence for pupils to practise, improve and then be asked to demonstrate. 'Observers, look out for and tell me where you could really see the swinging that helped to make these excellent sequences' and 'Performers, thank you very much for your non-stop, varied and exciting actions. Can any of you tell me where you felt the swing helping you the most?'

Final Floor Activity

Encourage pupils to choose a different partner from the one they worked with in the previous month's lesson. If the leader does a short run, then swings up into a jump to turn to face where they started from, they will need little space.

Lesson Plan 11 • 30 minutes
July

Emphasis on: *(a) sequences, and remembering and being able to repeat two or three simple actions to create a smooth, flowing performance; (b) arousing pleasure and a sense of fun from participation in vigorous and challenging activity.*

Floorwork
12 minutes

Legs

1   Using your legs only, can you make up a short sequence of your favourite ways to travel? Include a still start and finish.

2   Variety will come from different sorts of actions, from different ways to use your body parts, and from changes of direction.

3   If I watch you only, will I see the same two or three actions being repeated?

Body

1   Show me how you can go from a favourite, still body shape on to a different body part, then into a different shape or back to the same one.

2   Perform slowly so that I can see the linking movements clearly. (For example, roll, twist, lean, swing, jump, lower.)

3   I hope all your shapes are firm and clear with no lazy, sagging bodies, please!

Arms

1   As you travel on hands only, or on hands and feet, can you plan to show me an interesting pathway like a triangle or a square?

2   Once again, if I am watching you only, will I see a starting and a finishing position where you are standing still?

3   Variety can come from having back, side or front towards the floor; from different body shapes and directions; and from having different body parts leading the actions.

Apparatus Work
16 minutes

1   Use a simple step or jump to bring you on to a piece of apparatus. With a beautifully stretched body, step or jump off on to a mat, do a soft, squashy landing, then a smooth sideways roll. Now move to a new piece of apparatus.

2   Can you use your hands to lift, pull, lever or twist you on to the apparatus? Travel on the apparatus using hands and feet with varied actions, shapes and directions. As you leave the apparatus, make your hands important this time.

3   For the last apparatus part of our last lesson of the year, work freely at favourite ways of travelling on floor and apparatus. You can stay at one favourite piece, or use more than one piece, remembering the main actions on each so that you could repeat them for me. Off you go!

Final Floor Activity
2 minutes

Run and jump high with a stretched body shape. Run and jump high with a wide body shape. Run and jump high with your own choice of body shape, which might be stretched or wide again.

Teaching notes and NC guidance
Development over 4 lessons

Floorwork

Legs

1 'Short sequence' infers a still, well-controlled start; two or three linked and different ways to travel; and a still, neat finish position, so pupils do not need much space in which to perform.

2 'Using feet with variety' can mean feet together, separate or on one foot only; with straight, semi-bent or well-bent legs; on tiptoes, balls of feet or heels; walking, running, jumping, hopping, bouncing or skipping.

3 A demonstration, with half the class watching the other half, can have the observers looking for a short, repeating pattern of two or three actions which they can identify.

Body

1 As a reminder, the teacher can lead pupils through all the different shapes we normally see in Gymnastic Activities. 'Show me how you can go' challenges them to show good linking actions between the different shapes, moving from body part to body part.

2 A three-part sequence will be long enough for variety and to challenge pupils' planning of different supporting parts and links.

3 Words such as strong, firm, clear, beautifully stretched and hard-working should be used in praising and encouraging good work.

Arms

1 Each side of the triangle or square is only 2–3 metres, long enough to show the action two or three times before changing to the next one.

2 Encourage a standing, still position when starting and finishing to signal 'I have done it once through' before repeating it.

3 We want pupils to understand the pattern of thinking when planning for variety: What actions? What are body parts doing? What shapes am I showing clearly? Where am I doing it? In which directions?

Apparatus work

1 Up to, on to and almost immediately off the apparatus, with more time spent on the floor than on apparatus. The jump, land, sink to floor and roll sideways is the main part of the sequence, and there should be lots of potential demonstrators to call up.

2 Using hands to mount, now spend more time on the apparatus, travelling in a thoughtful, well-planned way which, ideally, you can remember and repeat.

3 The year's teaching will have been successful if the class use this final part of the apparatus work to demonstrate: (a) quiet, almost non-stop, vigorous activity, performed with great enthusiasm; (b) an unselfish, considerate sharing of the space in the interest of own and others' safety; (c) neat, well-controlled, versatile movements done whole-heartedly; (d) a sense of improved self-confidence due to the many achievements easily seen and recognised.

Final floor activity

One of the most marked improvements of the year will be pupils' ability to show good quality running, jumping and landing; to make clear body shapes; and to hold a still starting and finishing position.

Dance

Introduction to Dance

Dance has a special place in primary school Physical Education because it is intensely physical, sociable, co-operative, creative and expressive. Dance is also great fun and a source of enjoyment for pupils.

The lively, physical nature of Dance is particularly valuable now, when children's lives have become increasingly sedentary and inactive. Well-organised lessons should be vigorous, active and non-stop, because the actions being performed are natural and easy. There are none of the problems encountered when controlling Games implements. There is no potential break in the flow of the lesson as when organising Gymnastic apparatus. In Dance, the teacher should be able to make his or her lessons 'scenes of busy activity'.

It has been said 'If you have never created something, you have never experienced a true sense of contentment.' Creativity is an ever-present feature of Dance and the wise teacher will always recognise, share and praise such achievements.

Teachers with little interest in Physical Education often admit to being impressed by the amount of language heard, used, understood and learned by pupils during Physical Education lessons. This discovery has been a stimulus to those teachers in their subsequent teaching of the subject.

Happily, the 1999 revised version of the National Curriculum still requires schools to include both creative and traditional folk dance. The latter almost completely disappeared during the 1960s and 1970s when education lecturers called folk dance 'quite unsuitable' for primary school pupils because the steps and patterns 'belong to the adult world'.

Whether we are teaching creative or traditional dance, both teacher and class must have a definite 'goal' so that practising can become focused, repeatable, performable – and done expressively, with total commitment and involvement. The challenge to 'find ways to balance', for example, becomes much more exciting and 'real' when the outcome is the tightrope walker in the circus with all the dangerous, unsteady wobbling about in space.

The following lesson plans are designed to provide lots of ideas and practical help to the non-specialist class teacher. It recognises that each revised and reduced version of the NC provides less material, practical help and guidance regarding the content of dance and less help with the nature of good teaching practice in Physical Education. The Teacher Notes that accompany each lesson plan aim to translate Programme of Study, Attainment Target and Learning across the National Curriculum elements into easily understandable objectives as well as giving practical help and guidance with the understanding, organising and teaching of the lessons.

The aims of Dance

1 Dance is physical and we aim to make lessons physically challenging. The focus is on the body and the development of well-controlled, poised, versatile movement. Vigorous actions also develop strength and flexibility and promote normal, healthy growth and development.

2 Dance is creative and we aim to let pupils use their imagination. Using imagination and skill to plan and present something original makes Dance a most satisfying activity. When a pupil's capacity for creative thinking and action is recognised and appreciated by the teacher, and shared with the class, this can increase self-confidence and self-esteem.

3 Dance is expressive and communicative, and we aim to let pupils express their inner feelings through outward movement. We use our bodies to 'express and communicate ideas' (NC Programme of Study). Feelings are expressed through body movement, as in angry stamping of feet; joyful gesturing of arms – 'Goal!'; fear, with its tight withdrawal of the whole body; or the swaggering shoulders and strides of the over-confident.

4 Dance is artistic and we aim to include variety and contrasts in every lesson. Knowledge and understanding of the elements that enhance the quality of a performance need to be taught, and they contribute to a pupil's artistic education. Variety and contrast in the use of body action, shape, speed, force, level and direction are major contributors to improved quality.

5 Dance is sociable, friendly and co-operative and we aim to let pupils work alone, with a partner and in groups in a variety of roles. Because movement is natural, without the difficulty of controlling unpredictable Games implements, success is quickly achieved. This achievement is often shared with a partner or group, leading to a strong sense of 'togetherness'; unselfish sharing of space; taking turns; demonstrating to and being demonstrated to; and being appreciated by others' comments are all typical of Dance teaching.

6 Dance is fun and we aim to make enjoyment a constant feature. Enjoyment from being praised for achievement; from participating and interacting in such an interesting and sociable activity; and from feeling and looking better after exercise, can all have a significant influence on peoples' eventual choice of lifestyle in years to come.

The creative Dance lesson Plan

Warming-up activities aim to inspire an enjoyable, lively start to the lesson and put the class in the mood for Dance. The activities need to be simple enough to get the class working, almost immediately, often by following the teacher who calls out and demonstrates the activities, which do not need to relate to the main theme or emphasis of the lesson.

Some form of travelling, using the feet, is the usual warming-up activity, with a specific way of moving being asked for. It might be to demonstrate better use of space, greater variety, greater control, good poise and body tension, or simply an enthusiastic use of all body parts to warm up.

The teacher, here, is a stimulating 'purveyor of action' enthusiastically leading the whole class, often by example, into whole-hearted participation in simple activities, needing little explanation.

Teaching and developing movement skills and patterns to be used in the new dance follows the warm-up. Teaching methods include challenging, questioning, use of good demonstrations, and direct teaching:

a 'Kneel down and curl to your smallest shape. Show me how you can start to grow, very slowly. Are you starting with your back, head, shoulders, elbows or arms? Show me clearly how you rise to a full, wide stretched position.'

b 'How are the bubbles (made by teacher and pupils) moving? Where are they going? Floating gently, gliding smoothly, soaring from low to higher, sinking slowly?'

Here, the teacher is an educator, informing, challenging, questioning, using demonstrations and sometimes using direct teaching.

Creating and performing the dance finishes off the lesson:

a 'Slowly, start to grow and show me which parts are leading as you rise to your full, wide flower shape in our "Spring" dance. You might even twist your flower shape to look at the sun.'

b 'For our "Bubbles" dance, I will say the four actions that we have practised – floating, gliding, soaring, sinking – slowly, and you will show me how you have planned to dance them.'

The teacher, now, is a coach, helping and guiding the pupils as they work at their creation, moving around to all parts of the room to advise, encourage, enthuse, praise, and, eventually, present and lead the thanks to them for their demonstrations.

Depending on its complexity, a dance will be repeated two to four times to allow sufficient time for repetition, practice and improvement to take place, and a satisfactory performance to be achieved and presented.

Developing Dance Movement

To avoid confusion, the teacher will be thinking about, looking for, and talking about one element of movement at a time. In the early stages of a lesson's development, the teacher should only look at the actions and how the body parts concerned perform them. This allows an opportunity for progress and improvement. If, however, the teacher is exhorting the class to think about 'your spacing, actions, shape, speed – and what about some direction changes?', all at the same time, then confusion will be the only outcome.

Stage 1 The Body
What is the child doing?

1 Actions – travelling, jumping, turning, rolling, balancing, gesturing, rising, falling, etc.

2 Body parts – legs, feet, hands, shoulders, head, etc.

3 Body shape – stretched, curled, wide, twisted, arched.

Stage 2 The Space
Where is the child doing it?

1 Directions – forwards, backwards, sideways.

2 Level – high, medium, low.

3 Size – own, little, personal space; whole-room, large, general space, shared with others.

Stage 3 The Quality
How is the child doing it?

1   Weight or effort – firm, strong, vigorous, heavy.

2   Time or speed – sudden, fast, explosive, speeding up; slow, still, slowing down

Stage 4 The Relationships
With whom is the child doing it?

1   Alone – but always conscious of sharing space with others.

2   Teacher – near, following, mirroring, in a circle with, away from, back towards.

3   Partner – leading, following, meeting, parting, mirroring, copying, touching.

4   Group – circle, part of class for a demonstration.

Teaching Methods

Enthusiastic teaching is the main inspiration behind a successful lesson and usually creates an equally enthusiastic response in pupils.

The lesson plan is the busy teacher's essential guide. Failure to work from a written-down plan can result in repetition of lessons. July's lesson will only be more advanced than the previous September's if all the lessons in between have been recorded and referred to.

'Shared choice' or 'indirect' teaching is the lesson plan most often used. The teacher decides the nature of the activity and challenges the class to decide on the actions. 'As you travel and stop to my tambourine beat, can you show me varied travelling actions, and clear, still, body shapes?'

Shared choice teaching with its 'Can you show me…?' approach produces a wide variety of results to add to the repertoire of both class and teacher. The NC requirement that pupils should be able to demonstrate that they can plan and 'use skills, actions and ideas appropriately' is best achieved through shared choice.

'Direct' teaching takes place when the teacher tells the class what to do. For example: 'Skip to visit every part of the room…'; 'Stand with feet apart. Slowly stretch your arms high above your head.' If the class are restless, unresponsive or doing poor work, a directed activity can restore interest and discipline, and provide ideas and starting points from which to develop. Less creative pupils will benefit from direct teaching.

Pupil demonstrations are essential teaching aids because we remember what we see – good quality, safe, correct ways to perform, and good examples of variety and interesting contrasts. Occasional pupil demonstrations with follow-up comments by the observing pupils often bring out points not noticed by the teacher. Making friendly, encouraging, helpful comments to classmates is good for class morale and for extending the class repertoire.

'Be found working, not waiting' is a motto the class should have been trained to understand and pursue in order to enjoy satisfactory lessons with sufficient time for the creative dance, which is the climax of the lesson.

Praise and recognition of progress and good work are important teaching aids, particularly when given with enthusiasm. Words of praise should be specific because they are heard by all and remind the class of the main points: 'Well done, Emma. Your floating snowflake movement was light and gentle.'

It has been said that 'Dance is all about making, remembering and repeating patterns'. Whether we are performing a created dance or an existing folk dance, there will be a still start and finish and an arrangement of repeated parts within.

National Curriculum requirements for Dance – Key Stage 1: the main features

'The government believes that two hours of physical activity a week, including the National Curriculum for Physical Education and extra-curricular activities, should be an aspiration for all schools. This applies to all key stages.'

Programme of Study

Pupils should be taught to:

a use movement imaginatively, responding to stimuli, including music, and performing basic skills (e.g. travelling, being still, making a shape, jumping, turning, gesturing)

b change the rhythm, speed, level and direction of their movements

c create and perform dances using simple movement patterns, including those from different times and cultures

d express and communicate ideas and feelings.

Attainment Targets

Pupils should be able to demonstrate that they can:

a select and use skills, actions and ideas appropriately, applying them with co-ordination and control

b copy, explore, repeat and remember skills, and link them in ways that suit the activities

c talk about differences between their own and others' work; suggest improvements; and use this understanding to improve their performance.

Main NC Headings when considering assessment, progression and expectation

Planning – mostly before performing, but planning also takes place during performance, with pupils making quick decisions to find a space or adapt a skill. In these initial, exploratory stages, pupils try things out and learn from early efforts. When planning is satisfactory, there is evidence of understanding of the task; good use of own ideas; and consideration for others sharing the space.

Performing and improving performance – always the main outcome to be achieved. When performing is satisfactory, there is evidence of well-controlled, neat, safe and thoughtful work; a capacity for almost non-stop work, alone and with others; and simple skills being performed accurately and linked together with increasing control.

Linking actions – pupils build longer, 'joined-up' sequences of linked actions in response to the task set and stimuli used. In the same way that joined-up words make language and joined-up notes make music, joined-up actions produce movement sequences, ideally with a clear and obvious beginning, middle and end.

Reflecting and making judgements – pupils describe what they and others have done; talk about what they liked in a performance; and then make practical use of this reflection to improve. Where standards in evaluating are satisfactory, there is evidence of accurate observation and awareness of the actions; understanding of differences and similarities seen in demonstrations; awareness of key features and ways to achieve and improve them; and sensitive concern for others' feelings when discussing them.

Year 1 Dance programme

Pupils should be able to:

Autumn	Spring	Summer
1 Dress correctly; behave well; listen and respond quickly.	1 Respond whole-heartedly with vigour.	1 Be aware of good spacing, able to change direction to avoid impeding others, and for safety.
2 Find out movements possible in isolated body parts – head, spine, arms, hands, feet, legs.	2 Share space safely and unselfishly.	2 Develop skill, always trying to improve, working alone and with a partner.
3 Use whole-body movements to reach into all the space around self, still and travelling.	3 Neatly link actions together, with confidence and control.	3 Improve by making work neater, more varied, with changes of shape, direction, speed and effort.
4 Look for and travel to spaces, using and improving varied actions – walk, run, jump, skip, hop, bounce, slide, gallop.	4 Demonstrate skills, enhanced by using variety and contrasts.	4 Co-operate with a partner to decide how to plan to respond to a challenge whole-heartedly.
5 Co-operate with a partner, leading, following, copying.	5 Express ideas through movement, e.g. 'Winter' – freezing streams and melting, dripping icicles.	5 Respond rhythmically to music and percussion to perform short patterns of movement that can be repeated and remembered.
6 Respond enthusiastically and with imagination to challenges.	6 Create rhythmic patterns of joined-up movements that can be repeated.	6 Use contrasts, like variety, as a way of enhancing performance.
7 Celebrate Autumn with e.g. 'Autumn Leaves' and their windy day movements.	7 Be able to demonstrate contrasts in use of speed, shape and tension.	7 Perform dances with a poised start and finish, and a smooth, neatly linked-up middle.
8 Use vocal sounds to accompany e.g. 'Leaves' and 'Fireworks' dances.	8 Understand nature of 'Opposites' – heavy, light; strong, gentle – and express them in a partner dance.	8 Express nature's seasonal period of growth and birth through bodily movement.
9 Learn traditional dance steps and figures. Combine them in a four-part pattern in a simple set made up of single couples.	9 Learn simple movements and figures of traditional dance and use them with a partner.	9 Use vocal sounds rhythmically as stimuli to inspire and accompany movements.
10 Celebrate Christmas with e.g. 'Fairy in the Toyshop' and the clowns, robots and penguins being brought into action, one at a time, by the fairy's wand.	10 Respond to varied stimuli – music, objects and imagery, winter words, partners, opposites.	10 Express moods and feelings by body movement and develop them into a dance with a partner, 'Making a little pattern you can remember and repeat.'
11 Enjoy performing and observing, learning from own and others' comments on good quality work.	11 Continue to develop control and co-ordination in basic actions such as travelling, jumping, stillness and gesture.	11 Become a keen, appreciative observer of others' movements, keen, also, to learn from others.
	12 Be keen to practise, repeat, improve, remember and present a performance.	
	13 Try to 'feel' movement quality contrasts as in light, gentle travelling bubbles, and the hard, jagged frozen stream.	
	14 Be an interested spectator, and be encouraging by making helpful comments.	

Lesson Plan 1 • 25 minutes
September

Theme: *Space and body-shape awareness; controlled and rhythmic travelling and stopping in a quiet, responsive and co-operative environment.*

Warm-up Activities
4 minutes

1 All stand in a big circle, where we can see one another, with your feet apart for balance. Let us make circles with different body parts. Circle one shoulder forwards and back three times, then the other shoulder.

2 Bend one arm and circle your elbow forwards, up, and behind three times, then do the same with the other one.

3 Circle one long arm forwards, up, and behind three times, then the other long arm.

4 Let's do those three sets of circling again and try to make the circles even bigger by using your legs and body more, and reaching to spaces in the front and at the rear. Shoulder... elbow... arm.

Movement Skills Training
13 minutes

1 Somewhere in the room is an empty space for you to find and visit. Can you see it? Ready. Skip straight to it, pause, and show me a clear, big body shape. Go! Can your shape use a lot of space? Reach out far and spread yourselves. Keep still.

2 Look out for your next empty space. Creep to it and freeze into the smallest possible shape. Go! How is your body supported? On feet, knees, back or side? Are you using only a tiny amount of space?

3 Look around again for your next, near space. Run and jump into it and use lots of space for your big, wide body shape. Go!

4 Tiptoe to your next space and melt into the smallest shape. Go! Who is the tiniest, most curled-shape person?

Dance — Going and Stopping
8 minutes

1 In our 'Going and Stopping' dance, show me your best starting shape, which might show me what your first, lively travelling action will be. Then travel to a space and stop in the biggest shape you can make. Go!

2 Be still. Feel your body working hard to fill the space.

3 Look for your next space. Travel to it with a gentler action, like walking, sliding, gliding, creeping and show me your tiny shape, using hardly any of the space. Go!

4 Be still and tiny, whether on feet, knees, back, side or up-ended on your shoulders.

5 Relax and rest for a moment. Well done, travellers and shape makers.

6 From now on you will decide when to move on to your next space without a signal from me. It would be brilliant if you were able to do this in a nice, rhythmic way, saying to yourself 'I travel, travel, travel, then make a huge shape; I move, move, move and hold a small shape; I go, go, go and hold my best shape.' Begin.

7 What excellent large and tiny shapes! I like watching your varied travelling – some lively and some more gentle – and I like your varied shapes – the biggest possible and the tiniest possible. Keep working hard to show me the differences.

8 Half the class will watch the other half. Watchers, please look for and tell me about big and small shapes, neat travelling, and any rhythmic actions.

Dance

Teaching notes and NC guidance
Development over 2 lessons

Pupils should be taught to:

a respond readily to instructions. Direct teaching of specific activities in the warm-up should be accompanied by the whole class being seen to be active and responding. Direct teaching in the middle part of the lesson necessitates their listening carefully to the varied challenges. Anyone not listening is soon discovered. An enjoyable lesson with a variety of interesting material, taught and demonstrated by an enthusiastic teacher, is the best incentive to equally enthusiastic participation;

b be physically active. The onus is on the teacher to 'get on with it', with the minimum of long-winded explanations. 'Creep to your next space and freeze small. Go!' While there is a lot of freedom in the 'Going and Stopping' dance, the pace is dominated by the teacher moving pupils on from stage to stage – keeping them listening, attending, planning and responding;

c be aware of the safety risks of inappropriate clothing, footwear and jewellery. September is the time to lay down essential traditions for the way the new class dress, behave and respond in Physical Education lessons.

Warm-up Activities

1 An instant start with pupils watching and copying the teacher-leader to understand 'making circles with different body parts'.

2 The forwards, up, and back elbow circling is helped by one foot being in front of the other for a strong balanced base.

3 Opposite foot forward helps balance in long-arm circling forwards, up and back.

4 'Even bigger circles' means even better exercise for the seldom-used shoulder joints.

Movement Skills Training

1 From body parts awareness, they are being moved on to space awareness and body shape awareness, both in the whole room, and immediately around themselves.

2–4 Variety and contrasts in body actions, size, shape, and amount of force used, here, enhance the quality of a performance and teach the class what is good in good movement.

Going and Stopping Dance

1–4 The presentation of a still start with a clear, appropriate body shape; a neat, thoughtful, poised middle answering the set challenge ('lively travelling'; 'gentler action'); and a still finish, as requested ('with the biggest shape'; 'your tiny shape'), gives pupils a pattern that will continually be asked of them in their Dance lessons. It has been said that 'Dance is all about making, remembering and repeating patterns.' There will be a still start and finish and an arrangement of repeated parts within.

5–7 The short, different, individual patterns of lively travel with big shapes and gentler travel with small shapes are themselves combined in to one bigger, repeating pattern where the class are working hard to 'show the differences'.

8 In the half-watching-half climax of the lesson, praise will be for those whose contrasting body shapes, varied travelling and excellent use of space are evident.

Lesson Plan 2 • 25 minutes
September

Theme: *Body parts awareness.*

Warm-up Activities
5 minutes

1 Find a big space where you can see me and move without touching anyone. Put your feet apart for good balance and reach high with both arms. Bend your arms, neck, back, waist, knees and ankles until you are crouched down with your hands on the floor. Now, stretch up your ankles, knees, waist, back, neck and shoulders and finish with your arms high above your head again. (Repeat several times, bending, stretching and thinking about the joints concerned.)

2 Let's move around now, singing and making these actions together:

*If you're happy and you know it, clap your hands,
If you're happy and you know it, clap your hands,
If you're happy and you know it, and you really want to show it,
If you're happy and you know it, clap your hands.*

*If you're happy and you know it, stamp your feet,
. . . bend your knees . . . wave your hands . . . shake all over.*

Movement Skills Training
12 minutes

1 Show me happy travelling actions to visit all parts of the room.

2 Stop a minute and look at these four happy travellers and their skipping, galloping, bouncing, running and jumping.

3 Find a partner for 'Follow my Leader' with each of you showing the other your happy travelling actions. You might use some of the good ideas we have just seen. Watch your partner's feet, legs and whole body and try to copy and follow. Change leader when I call 'Change!' Off you go.

4 Now, stand facing your partner. Show me these friendly hand actions. Wave one hand; wave the other hand; clap both hands, gently, 1, 2, 3, 4, starting high and coming down, down, down to just in front of you both. Wave, wave; clap, clap, clap, clap.

5 Let's keep a nice slow rhythm this time – wave, wave; clap, 2, 3, 4; high wave, high wave; high claps, both hands, lower and lower. Friendly wave and wave; friendly claps, claps, claps, stop!

Dance — Follow My Leader
8 minutes

1 Partners, stand ready, one behind the other. When I call 'Travel!' the leader will show his or her lively, happy travelling for the partner to copy. When I call 'Stop!', partners face each other, ready to wave and clap. Let's take it to there. Travel!... Stop!

2 Try not to lose your partner by rushing ahead too far. Show your partner neat feet and leg actions to copy. Stand ready now for the other one to lead when I call 'Travel!'

3 Travel! Look for spaces, leaders, please, and keep repeating your one or two actions.

4 Stop! Face each other and show me your waves and your handclaps at a nice, slow speed – wave, wave; clap, clap, clap and stop!

5 Well done, new leaders and followers. In our next practice you will decide when to change from travelling to waving and clapping and when to start travelling again. All ready? Begin.

6 First leader leading; stop and face each other; other leader leading.

Dance

Teaching notes and NC guidance
Development over 2 lessons

Improvement comes with thoughtful, focused practice and repetition of, ideally, rhythmic movement. Good practice for this is the warm-up activity with its repeating, rhythmic movements keeping everyone together with the teacher. In 'Follow My Leader' we want the leader to be aware of the two or three repeating travelling actions being performed so that they can be remembered, repeated and improved.

The teacher-directed 'Wave, wave; clap, 2, 3, 4; high wave, high wave; slow claps, 2, 3, 4' means that pupils do not have to remember this as well as their travelling. All can be kept together and reinforced as the teacher rhythmically accompanies the actions.

Another incentive to focused, thoughtful planning and improving is the tradition of presenting half of the class to the other half in a demonstration followed by comments. All then know that they will be looked at.

Warm-up Activities

1 All can see and hear the teacher leading them, in this instant 'Follow me, the leader' start to the lesson. To reinforce the 'Body-parts awareness' aspect of the lesson, the class can be asked to say the parts concerned as they bend and stretch them, slowly, together.

2 An action words song is always popular and can be expanded by asking 'Who can suggest a pair of actions we can now include?' (for example, twist and wave; bend and stretch; clap and bounce.)

Movement Skills Training

1, 2 Instant start. Short explanation; start music; go! The demonstrations give new ideas to those who might only have been running and jumping.

3 Emphasise that the leader is expected to show at least two actions which are being repeated so that the follower can eventually travel in unison with the leader. The need to keep listening for the signal 'Change!' (of leader) ensures their continued attention and good behaviour.

4, 5 The teacher and a partner should demonstrate the waves and claps, after which the teacher calls out the sensible timing for all to follow.

Follow My Leader Dance

1–4 The teacher's 'Travel!' and 'Stop!' aim to tell pupils what is a good distance to travel as leader. Pupils travel too far, usually, if undirected. 'Three or four travelling actions are enough, ideally into a good space, to spread yourselves for the waving and the clapping.'

5, 6 Pupils now have to decide: a) how far to travel, before stopping and turning to face each other; b) the speed, and places in space, to wave, wave, clap, 2, 3, 4; before c) turning to follow a new leader. This becomes an exciting, interesting and action-filled dance with some following the first leader; some turning, to face each other; some waving; some clapping; and some, off travelling again, following the new leader.

Class teachers should emphasise the value of this friendly, sociable, co-operative partners dance at the start of a new school year.

Lesson Plan 3 • 25 minutes
October

Theme: *Autumn.*

Warm-up Activities
5 minutes

1 Our dance is going to be about 'Autumn Leaves'. Show me any kind of flying actions to visit all parts of the room.

2 Stay where you are, just like a helicopter, hovering, gently up and down, lifting and turning and floating. Good.

3 Glide straight across the room. Tilt over to one side to turn. Glide, zoom straight, turn with a lean, and let one wing go higher than the other. Good. You all look beautifully streamlined.

4 Fly like a glider, going down, down at speed and then up. This is called 'soaring'. Keep your wide wings shape. Soar down and up.

5 Well done, flyers. All come in and land now, please, and look at what I collected last night.

Movement Skills Training
12 minutes

1 These fallen leaves have all blown down from their trees in the last few days. Watch what happens when I throw one in the air.

2 What did it do? Yes, it floated, twisted down – but not in a straight line. It even seemed to hang in the air at one point.

3 Still sitting, lift your hands up high and let me see your fingers gently falling to the floor, twisting, turning, hanging, then falling without a sound, like a leaf.

4 Change to kneeling to give your leaf a higher start and let you do a bigger body move in front, to one side, or even behind you. Let your fingers start in a shape of one of my leaves that you like. Are you crinkly, wide, flat, long, twisted or jagged? Surprise me with interesting flying movements.

5 Start the movement very high, standing on tiptoes, almost as high as some of the trees where the leaves started. As your fingers drift, float, twist and turn, falling, your whole body will need to lower, settle and try to melt into the floor, very carefully with no bumps. Please practise.

6 All stand and let me hear you making a gentle wind noise to start your leaf fluttering. The wind gets stronger and louder and you fly off into space, twisting, turning, hovering, gliding.

7 The wind noise dies away and your leaf slowly falls to the ground, rolling over, two or three times. Is your body shape the same as your hands were at the start?

Dance — Autumn Leaves
8 minutes

1 Half of the class sit down around the outside of the room, ready to make sounds as they blow, like the wind, gently, strongly, then gently. The other half prepare to float up and down; then snap away into space, flying, gliding, soaring; then settling to land and roll along the ground to rest and show their final shape.

2 Change places. Wind makers, a gentle light wind to start, please.

3 Now, it's a very stormy, loud wind. Leaves make big, disturbed movements, then the storm passes, the wind sound softens and the leaves fall gently, rolling over and over on the ground. If you are an unusual-shaped leaf, I might pick you up to show you off!

4 One more turn each, then we can discuss any performances that we particularly enjoyed, and try to explain why we liked them.

Dance

Teaching notes and NC guidance
Development over 3 lessons

'Pupils should be taught to use contrasts of speed, shape, direction and level.'

This lesson helps pupils develop these three qualities:

○ **Speed:** observing a leaf falling from a height, or imagining it falling from a high tree, will inspire descriptive words such as 'floating; turning; hovering; gliding; soaring; swooping; dropping; falling', all of which provide practice in using contrasts of speed
○ **Shape:** observing a group of leaves brought into class will inspire descriptive words such as 'curly; flat; crinkly; wide; long; twisted; jagged' and will provide excellent images for the body to practise and feel
○ **Direction and level:** leaves glide straight ahead; drop and then soar to a higher level; are buffeted from side to side by the wind; hang momentarily, then are blown backwards to where they came from, before dropping down, down to the ground.

Leaves provide excellent images because they are so common and because of the variety of interesting ways in which they can move.

Warm-up Activities

1 An instant start, after only a five-second introduction. Instant starts get lessons off to a good start. While the class practise, the teacher can praise and spread good flying ideas with comments on the varied flying actions – the gliding, turning, weaving, leaning, soaring.

2 In their own space, pupils now practise and feel the floating, hovering, turning, more gentle helicopter or floating, leaf-like actions.

3, 4 The speedier soaring with wings spread wide, using the whole room, needs to be done with care, to avoid crashes. 'Look for good, big spaces as you fly to all parts of the room.'

5 Well-warmed and well-practised for later in the lesson, the class are now shown the leaves collected by the teacher so that leaf shapes and flying actions can be observed closely.

Movement Skills Training

1–5 The teacher's questioning and the observing of the leaves in flight inspire an awareness of the types of rising, floating, falling movements, as well as the very different shapes that can lead to different flight patterns.

6, 7 Own vocal sounds, with the wind-like accompaniment growing in intensity from light and gentle to loud and strong, then back to quietly dying away, provide the three stages – fluttering gently; breaking off vigorously and flying away; and slowly falling to the ground and rolling over – of a typical autumn leaf on a windy day.

Autumn Leaves Dance

1–3 Half of the class sit around the outside of the room, looking in at and making vocal sounds for the dancing half, in this three-stage dance which is inspired by the varying intensity of the vocal sounds accompaniment. Gentle wind; stormy wind; softening wind. Many of the final leaf shapes on the ground will be like those presented by the teacher at the start of the lesson.

4 As well as discussing good dance performances after the second practices, good accompanying vocal sounds deserve a complimentary mention because of their huge contribution to the lesson.

Lesson Plan 4 • 25 minutes
November

Theme: *Sounds that inspire and accompany actions.*

Warm-up Activities
5 minutes

1   Cross your arms so that your hands rest on the opposite shoulder. Take slow, giant, noisy strides and slap your shoulders noisily. Slow, loud, giant strides; 1, 2, 3, 4; slow, slow, 3 and stop!

2   Now, something completely different. Up on tiptoes for tiny, fast, pitter-patter steps. Hands quickly and gently slap sides of thighs. Fast–go! Step, step, step, step, 5, 6, 7, 8; quick, quick, quick, quick, 5, 6, 7 8; slap legs, slap legs, 5, 6, 7, 8. That was fast! Good.

3   Find a partner and stand one behind the other. Try the giant, slow strides with claps and the tiny, fast steps with slaps. Leaders, ready? Go! Slow, slow, slow, slow; quick, 2, 3, 4, 5, 6, 7, 8; slow, slow, loud steps; quick, quick, quiet steps, 5, 6, 7, 8. Well done. Change places and show me the different actions and sounds.

Movement Skills Training
12 minutes

1   With me, all say the words on my card. Listen to how they sound different to each other:

- ○ **SIZZLE!** Show me how something might move if it's sizzling. Say it again. What does it make you think of? (Fuse of a firework; sausages frying.)
- ○ **ZOOM!** What sort of action will this be? Slow or quick? Gentle or lively? What could it be? (Rocket; motorcycle.)
- ○ **WHOOSH!** This sounds a bit like the wind sounds we made last month, doesn't it? In addition to the wind, what might it be?
- ○ **BANG!** What sort of action would 'Bang' be? (Firework exploding, scattering into space, opening out.)

2   Practise moving to these words and saying them. Try to show me the speed and the force you feel is right for each word.

3   If you see pictures in your head as you do the actions, that will help you to make the movements more 'real'.

4   Have a last practice. Put your whole voice into the words and your whole body into the actions.

Dance — Sizzle! Zoom! Whoosh! Bang!
8 minutes

1   Those were very exciting sounds and actions. Can we look first at all those whose sounds have been used to accompany fireworks – probably a rocket! Show the sizzling fuse; the zooming start; the whooshing up into space; and the big bang explosion, with all the scattering of parts. Go! (Watch; comment.)

2   Well done. I hope any real rockets you see will be as splendid as yours. Now, let's have a look at the others whose actions were used to show something other than fireworks. We will watch them carefully and guess what they are showing us. (Watch; guess; make helpful comments.)

3   All keep practising your exciting actions with your own sound. Show me clear actions, good shapes and speed and a good finish.

Dance

Teaching notes and NC guidance
Development over 3 lessons

'Physical Education should involve the pupils in planning.'

Following the introductory class discussion about the nature of the four words and what sort of actions they might inspire, the imaginative planning of ways to use, co-ordinate and express the words in action begins. Good use of the elements emphasised in the previous lesson – contrasts of speed, shape, direction and level – will enhance the quality, variety and contrast of the eventual performance.

Positive personal qualities such as enthusiasm, imagination and willingness to work hard at a challenge are evident in some of the outstanding planning that takes place, as is a willingness to listen to and adapt to the views of a partner.

While most demonstrations display good ideas for neat, controlled, versatile movement which had to be planned, demonstrations in this lesson also display highly individual, surprising and exciting ideas for others to see and try.

Warm-up Activities

1   As is often the case, the teacher's accompanying 'rhythmicising' reminder of the actions and their speeds ensures a quick, attentive start with pupils all listening for the noisy actions.

2   Once again, feet and hands are both involved in the sound making, but at a completely different speed and size. Tiny, quiet, quick steps and equally tiny, quick hand slaps on thighs now contrast with the earlier, big, noisy shoulder slaps and loud, giant strides.

3   In this challenging follow-the-leader partner work, where giant, slow, loud, striding and clapping alternate with tiny, fast, quiet, stepping and slapping, partners who can work, almost mirroring each other, in unison, will deserve to be shown to the class.

Movement Skills Training

1–4 After saying the words along with the teacher and one another, the class then try to show each object and action that they identify as belonging to the sound. In addition to the obvious and seasonal fireworks, some classes will produce a range of completely unexpected responses. The words can be shortened or elongated for interest and to match quick or very slow actions. The quick 'BANG!' of a gun, for example, can contrast with the slow

'WHOO-OO-OO-SH!' of a gardener's hose spraying water over a large area. Pupils decide and practise the action; improve it by applying the right amount of speed and force; and do everything (vocal sounds and movements) in a whole-hearted, eye-catching way.

Sizzle! Zoom! Whoosh! Bang! Dance

1   Those celebrating the seasonal fireworks work as a group to demonstrate their expressiveness and their understanding of the essential quality of such November 5th movement.

2–3 Those who have surprised and delighted the teacher with their exciting and unexpected ideas and creativity are observed in small groups and the others guess what they are showing.

Lesson Plan 5 • 25 minutes
November/December

Theme: *Simple, traditional dance steps and figures.*

Warm-up Activities
5 minutes

1   Listen to this country-dance music and count its rhythm with me. 1, 2, 3, 4, 5, 6, 7, 8. This time, clap and count with me.

2   Skip to the music and see if our clapping is still keeping in time with the music. Skip, 2, 3, 4, clapping, clapping, 7, 8. Keep going, 3, 4, clap and skip, 7 and stop!

3   I am going to divide the class into ones and twos. Number ones, you will skip in and out of the twos who are standing still. Do this for eight of my counts and then we change over. Ready, ones? Go! Number ones skip, 3, 4, around the twos, 7, 8; twos skip all around, 5, 6, 7, 8; ones again, 3, 4, skip, skip, 7, 8; twos go, 3, 4, skipping, skipping, 7, 8. (Demonstrate with dancers whose movements are neat, quiet, and in time with the music.)

Teach Steps and Figures of the Lesson's Folk Dance
14 minutes

1   All the number ones stand in a line down this side, please. Raise your arms sideways to keep you away from the person standing next to you. You need lots of space in your line.

2   Number twos stand in a line facing the number ones and you will be opposite a partner, about two big steps apart. We are all now standing in what is called a long set in country dancing.

3   Country dancing is very friendly, so step forwards and say 'Hello!' to your partner. Then step back into your long, straight line. Once again, forwards, 'Hello!' and back again.

4   Number twos, stand still, because ones are going to walk around you, and back to their own places. There's no hurry, ones. You have eight counts to do it. Ready? Walk around your partner, 3, 4, back to own line, 7, 8. Good. Nearly everyone got there. Again, ones, to make it perfect. 1, 2, around your partner, cross back, 7, 8.

5   That was brilliant. Number twos, you have seen it twice. Go around your partner, 3, 4, back to place, 7, 8. Again. Number twos, travel, travel, 3, 4, around, across, and back to place. Good.

6   Join both hands with your partner. All face the platform end of the room where the music is. We are going to skip for four counts, turn, with hands still joined, turn and skip back to your own places. Ready... skip forwards, 3 and turn; skip back into your places. Once again, join hands... skip, skip, 3 and turn; skip back to your places.

Dance — Long Set With Partners
6 minutes

Music: any lively, 32-bar English or Scottish dance tune

Formation:	One long set, partners about two metres apart.
Bars 1–8:	Both advance, shake hands, say 'Hello!' and go back to your own places.
Bars 9–16:	Ones dance across set, go around behind their partners, and back to own places.
Bars 17–24:	Twos repeat, going around behind partners, and then back to own places.
Bars 25–32:	Partners join hands, face the top of the set, and skip forwards for four; turn and skip back to places, for four. Repeat.

Dance

Teaching notes and NC guidance
Development over 2 lessons

'Pupils should be taught to be physically active.'

Folk-dance lessons are among the most physically demanding. The steps are lively and we can practise and repeat them, without stopping, for several groups of the eight-bar phrases of music typical of most English and Scottish folk dances. The simple figures, involving one couple, are easy to teach after a brief demonstration and explanation, and for most of this dance everyone is involved non-stop. As before, vocal rhythmic accompaniment of the actions keeps the whole class working together. 'Ones behind twos, 3, 4; back to own places, 7, 8; twos go round ones, 3, 4; back to own places, 7 and 8.'

The 'planning' that was emphasised in the previous lesson is equivalent to the thinking ahead here, to be doing the right thing at the right times, particularly if the teacher stops his or her vocal accompaniment to check if the class can remember the different parts of the dance.

Warm-up Activities

1, 2 This eight-count phrasing, typical in folk-dance music, is often used for warm-ups to Dance lessons, usually accompanied by some travelling actions. The quickish speed is very good and easy for young dancers. Slower music is much more difficult to dance to.

3 An eight-count travel is quite long and gives plenty of time to travel to many parts of the room, and around several of the stationary dancers. Skipping and going around and in and out of others is good practice for the many direction changes used in country dancing.

Teach Steps and Figures of the Lesson's Folk Dance

1, 2 The formation of a set for the first time can be helped if there are lines on the hall floor for one of the lines of dancers to stand on. Or number ones can be asked to 'Stand in line with the piano (or middle of door, etc.)'.

3–6 The teacher and one of the dancers demonstrate each of the four figures of the dance. Then all the couples practise that figure, accompanied by the teacher's chanting of the actions as a reminder of the timing and what to do.

Long Set With Partners Dance

Bars 1–8 In the 'both advance', beginners can walk in and more experienced dancers can skip with the traditional travelling step. A handshake on 'Hello!' or 'Hello! Hello!' is friendly, leaving four counts to use to take you back to your own place. Emphasise 'Be back after four counts, not too early or too late.'

Bars 9–16 Eight counts for this short travel is helped by 'Across for 2, halfway on 4, back to own side, 7 and 8.' Aim to have them behind their partners on count 4 only. (It helps them prepare for the next and final part of the dance if number ones move into the middle of the set to meet their number two partners early to join hands ready to do the skip forwards to the top of the set and back again to own places.)

Bars 17–24 'Skip and skip, turn on 3 and 4; skip and skip, back to own places on 8' ensures that they are in the right places at the right time, ready to re-start the whole dance for bars 25–32.

Lesson Plan 6 • 25 minutes
December

Theme: *Christmas.*

Warm-up Activities
4 minutes

1 All crouch down in a big space, well away from everyone. Listen to my poem and join in the actions:

   Jack in the box jumps up like this,
   Makes me laugh as he waggles his head,
   I gently press him down again,
   Saying 'Get in the box! You must go to bed!'

2 Help me with the words this time, please, as you do the actions. Show me the difference between the sudden, quick spring up and the slow squeeze down again. What funny waggling of your head will you do to make me laugh? Ready? *'Jack in the box jumps up...'.* (Demonstrate good examples of quick and slow contrasts.)

Movement Skills Training
13 minutes

1 Stand tall and proud like a fairy on a small platform. Show me how you will turn on the spot with tiny steps, like a dancer.

2 One hand will hold your magic wand and the other arm is used to balance you as you take your tiny, tiptoes, turning steps.

3 As you turn, your arms can go up and down. If I count to four, try to do one complete turn. Tiptoes turning for 1, 2, 3 and 4. Now, back the other way, tiptoes turning, 3, 4.

4 Let's all stand, floppy, like a circus clown, then jump up like a jack in the box. Try a funny walk, staggering forwards, back, side to side, throwing your arms in the air. Then pretend to throw a pail of water at someone. Stagger forwards, back, side to side, throw water.

5 Stiffen up now, robots, swinging your long straight arms and legs and doing sudden changes of direction, 1, 2, 3, quick spin turn. Keep your head looking straight ahead. If you want to see to one side, turn your whole body to face that way. Walk, walk, walk, turn.

6 Penguins, keep your flippers down at your sides, making small swimming movements. Walk tall, but lean from side to side as you go. Waddle, waddle, waddle; flippers, flippers, flippers.

Dance — Fairy In The Toyshop
8 minutes

1 Steve, will you come to the middle and dance as the fairy who is going to do a complete turn, then point the wand to make a group come alive. The next turn and point by the fairy stops that group. Let's all dance as clowns, then robots, then penguins, being started and stopped by Steve's magic wand. Steve, please begin. (A pattern for each group is encouraged. Clowns spring up; stagger forwards, back, side to side, throw water. Robots forwards, forwards, spin; forwards, forwards, spin. Penguins, waddle, waddle, waddle, flippers, flippers, flippers.)

2 Thank you, Steve, and well done all you toys. Sarah, will you be the fairy, starting and stopping each of the three separate groups I have now organised. Clowns, then robots, and then penguins, keep an eye on Sarah for your start and stop signals. When you are not dancing, watch the dancing group and tell me about any brilliant ideas you have seen.

Dance

Teaching notes and NC guidance
Development over 3 lessons

'Pupils should be able to show that they can show control in linking actions together in ways that suit the activities.'

Being able to plan simple skills and perform them as joined-up actions, neatly and with control, is a main requirement of the National Curriculum. Endlessly doing the same action, either on the spot or as a way to travel, is as inappropriate and pointless as writing one word or playing one note would be. From the very earliest stage, pupils should have been made aware that a sequence or pattern of movements requires at least two joined-up actions.

When the two or more actions being practised show variety and contrast, the teacher should be heard identifying the good things seen. 'Well done, Susan. Your floppy clown looked like it had no bones or muscles. Your sudden spring up surprised me with lots of muscles working.'

Clowns, robots and penguins will each be guided into practising and repeating a two- or three-part pattern of movement associated with these well-known images. The whole dance itself follows a repeating pattern as each of the groups is started and stopped in turn.

Warm-up Activities

1, 2 The teacher can say each line by him or herself, and then ask the class to join in, saying it a second time, thinking about and doing the actions being said. The 'jump up' action is a great favourite with lots of upward explosions. 'What funny waggling will you do?' is a challenge guaranteed to inspire many responses. The 'being squeezed down' ending calms them all down to stillness, ready for the next practice.

Movement Skills Training

1–3 All, in their good spaces, pretend to be balanced on a small platform, to perform an action all will have seen in a toy, rotating with arms rising and falling, with a wand.

4 The floppy clown, doing the jump up already practised, is another well-known favourite. The funny walk, staggers and throwing of water, is an excellent example of a 'joined-up actions' sequence.

5 The robot can travel stiffly forwards for three counts, then turn, equally rigidly, to face and go back to where it started from. Once again, this is a two-part repeating sequence.

6 The large, metronome-like travelling movement of the penguins, from side to side, accompanies their contrasting, small flippers swimming actions.

Fairy In The Toyshop Dance

1 Everyone dances all three parts of the dance, being started and stopped by the fairy's wand. The teacher's accompanying commentary, reminders and timings keep them all together and working hard to improve and fill the room with lively and impressive action.

2 A new fairy now starts and stops each of the three group actions in turn. The two groups not involved watch the different actions while the dancers are watching Sarah. The lesson's emphasis on 'joined-up actions' applies to all groups, including the two fairies.

Lesson Plan 7 • 25 minutes
January

Theme: *Winter.*

Warm-up Activities
4 minutes

All stand well spaced, where you can see me. I will sing the words slowly so that you can join in, saying the words as well as doing the actions, which must be big and lively.

This is the way we try to keep warm,
try to keep warm, try to keep warm, (running on the spot with high knee raising and big arm swinging)
this is the way we try to keep warm,
on a cold and frosty morning.

This is the way we bend and stretch,
bend and stretch, bend and stretch, (feet wide, bend and stretch knees and arms high)
this is the way we bend and stretch,
on a cold and frosty morning.

Movement Skills Training
13 minutes

1 Show me the gentle swirling waters of a stream as it trickles, curving around a bend or bubbling over stones. Let your whole body be part of the curving and the turning.

2 Slowly the frost comes down. The stream slows, freezes and stops. Show me your different jagged shapes becoming hard and spiky.

3 Here comes the sun, and the ice softens, loses its hard, jagged shape and starts, slowly at first, to flow again.

4 Near the stream is a house with water drip, drip, dripping down from the snow on the roof. With your fingers and arms, show me what this long trickling, dripping water looks like.

5 The frost comes and the dripping water slowly turns into a long, hard, stiff, jagged icicle. Show me! Drip again... freeze! Make your long, thin, frozen, still shapes. Feel hard and stiff.

6 Here comes the sun. The icicles start to smooth out, lose their sharpness and drip, drip, drip again in that long, wriggly line.

Dance — Frosty Winter
8 minutes

1 Half of the class will move like the little stream, all around the room. The other half stay in their places, to move like the water dripping down from the roof. Show me your starting shape.

2 Streams, flow slowly, curving, trickling, twisting, with your whole body working as you flow.

3 Rooftop trickles, start to drip, drip, drip in a long, thin line as you fall to the ground, plop, plop, plop.

4 The frost comes and the drips from the house turn into icicles, long, thin, hard, jagged shapes.

5 The stream starts to slow down, freeze and become solid. Hold your stiff, jagged shapes, which will be wider and flatter than the long, thin icicles.

6 Everyone, feel stiff and firm. If I push you, I should not be able to make you move.

7 Here comes the sun and we all start, very slowly at first, to melt, trickle, move along and then flow normally again.

8 The stream will demonstrate its movements first, then we will look at the melting snow.

9 Observe; comment; change over actions; practise; perform; observe.

Dance

Teaching notes and NC guidance
Development over 3 lessons

'Pupils should be involved in performing and improving performance.'

Desirable features of a successful performance include whole-hearted and vigorous activity, sharing space sensibly and unselfishly, with a concern for one's own and others' safety; neatly linking actions together with control; and showing skilfulness, variety and contrast.

Throughout this lesson, larger-than-life body movements are being used to express aspects of Winter. In the shared choice teaching method used, the teacher suggests the nature of the activity and the pupils decide the exact actions. 'Can you make your whole body bubble, curve and turn like the stream?' 'Show me what the long, dripping, trickling, melting snow looks like.' The dancer is using actions, shapes, rhythms and patterns to give a performance expressing 'Frosty Winter'.

Each group's demonstration of their half of the dance will help the other half with planning ideas when they change over. We remember what we see.

Warm-up Activities

Pupils can be asked, as part of the third lesson's development, to come along prepared to 'suggest other ways in which we might keep warm.' (For example, *This is the way we chase outside; dance in the hall; run fast and jump.*)

Movement Skills Training

1   Dance's enormous contribution to language development is evident here as the pupils hear, feel, experience at first hand, and come to understand the meanings of so many action words.

2, 3   The effects of frost on a stream in winter is an excellent, easy to understand image. The addition of different speeds, body tensions and shapes makes work in this dance more 'real'.

4–6   The next image – water dripping from snow on a roof, then freezing, then thawing – also makes what they are doing come alive in their imagination as they plan to express what 'Frosty Winter' can mean.

Frosty Winter Dance

1–3   The planning, practising and improving of the middle part of the dance, mean that two groups can start the created dance climax part of the lesson together. Their contrasting movements include the travelling actions of the stream, and the on-the-spot dripping of water from the roof. These movements are free, flowing, trickling, unrestrained.

4–6   The free-flowing drips from the roof, and the swirling, bubbling water in the stream, gradually change as the frost makes them hard, jagged, stiff and still with a tight body shape.

7   Into the tightly held, rigid stillness of the frosty setting, the sunshine comes and, slowly at first, the melting trickling stream and the melting rooftop snow start to flow again.

8, 9   In observing the stream group, and then the snow on the roof group, the two halves of the class are asked to look for, and comment on, expressive actions, changing tension and speed, and good, clear body shapes. Groups can change over parts in the following week.

Lesson Plan 8 • 25 minutes
January/February

Theme: *Heavy and light, strong and gentle, and the amount of tension used in the muscles.*

Warm-up Activities
4 minutes

1   Stand with your feet wide apart, giving you a strong grip to the floor. Bend your knees and arms and show me your strongest push by both hands up to the ceiling. Hold your wide, strong stretch!

2   Now feel as if you have no muscles in your arms, body or legs, and flop down – go! Stay hanging down, all floppy and loose.

3   Now firm up again and feel all those strong muscles lifting, twisting, pushing you up to the ceiling. Hold it firmly!

4   Suddenly relax, let go and – flop! (Repeat several times.)

Movement Skills Training
12 minutes

1   Feel strong in your legs and let me hear you running, beating the floor as firmly and quickly as you can, on your own spot. Go!

2   Pretend you are making huge splashes in a puddle. Splash, splash, splash, splash, heavy feet, pushing firmly.

3   Now pretend you are gently walking through a pool of water, trying not to make any splashes. Tiptoe, tiptoe, softly, softly.

4   Tiptoe so softly that your magic feet might even tip toe on top of the water. Gently, gently.

5   There's a big heavy weight in front of you that needs to be moved. It's blocking your way. Bend your knees and push it with your arms, shoulders, back and legs. Heave! Feel your strong muscles.

6   In front of you, now, is a huge balloon. Push it lightly away and walk along behind it, push, push, pushing it so gently that it doesn't fly away from you. Fingertips, fingertips, easy flicking.

7   Show me how your huge balloon might float along if it were being gently pushed by you. It will be slow, silent, rising and falling, sometimes turning, sometimes hanging, still, in the air.

Dance – Light and Heavy Opposites
9 minutes

1   Find a partner and plan an 'Opposites' dance. For example, one of you might start by pushing a heavy weight, your partner, slowly and with difficulty straight along the floor. The person being pushed will be heavy, firm, near to the floor. Then you change over. The one being pushed becomes the pusher and the partner becomes a big, light, easy-to-move balloon. Pushing is easy and the travelling is light and floating. You choose. Try my idea or one of your own.

2   Big splashes in the puddle, side by side, followed by tiptoeing on water might be another idea, with more travelling to do.

3   Punch, punch, punch, punch, heavy, strong movements against one partner (no contact!) sends that partner slowly stumbling backwards, step by step. In the opposite direction, the partner, now moving forwards, can gently flick a speck of dust in the air backwards with little bouncy steps.

4   Sit down, please. I have given you some ideas and many of you have planned your own ideas. We'll look at half of the class at a time, performing their favourite and best 'Opposites' dance. Look for and tell me about couples who change well from heavy to light, strong to gentle, with good, clear actions.

Dance

Teaching notes and NC guidance
Development over 3 lessons

'Pupils should be taught to try hard to improve and consolidate performances, alone, with a partner, and in a group.'

The teacher in Physical Education is fortunate that the lessons are so visual, allowing the whole class to be seen performing. Assessment of pupils' achievement and progress is of an overall performance, not the isolated parts that combine to make it. The finished piece of dance is the 'performance' referred to in the above requirements.

If 'Dancing is about using your imagination', the teacher begins by explaining the theme to the class, giving them good images to stir their imaginations. The use of images in the middle part of the lesson helps the class to work more quickly and with understanding. Partners will plan their own images and 'pictures in their head' as they respond to the challenge to plan and perform an 'Opposites' dance as the outcome of the topic's development.

Imagery inspires the actions, making them specific and clear. A rhythmic pattern of joined-up movements helps partners repeat, improve and remember their dance. Encouraging, helpful observations from both teacher and class lead to further progress and feelings of pleasure and enhanced confidence.

Warm-up Activities

1, 2 The teacher starts by putting the class 'in the picture' regarding the aims of this new lesson. 'We will be learning to understand, feel, and show the meanings of heavy and light, strong and gentle body tensions in our new Dance lesson.' Straight away, the contrast between a strong, firm, upwards drive from feet to upstretched arms, held body, and the floppy, hanging, limp, collapsed whole body, is felt.

3, 4 As well as the contrast in force between the firm, held, rigid shape and the floppy, loose, hanging shape, there is the added contrast in speed between the gradual, slow push upwards, and the sudden, quick collapse.

Movement Skills Training

The series of feeling: strong in the legs, running on the spot; firm with heavy feet, splashing in a puddle; gentle, on tiptoes, walking without splashing in a pool of water; solid as you push against the heavy weight; and light-fingered, pushing the balloon gently, provides the class with a variety of clear, easy-to-picture images through which to understand and experience examples of the different amounts of body tension that can be applied in movement.

Light and Heavy Opposites Dance

Pupils are now aware of what is meant by 'Opposites' in the amount of effort and force used in Dance movement. They have all practised and experienced at first hand the differences between: strong and gentle; firm and floppy; gradual and sudden; heavy and light. A challenge to plan a partner dance on 'Opposites', or to use examples given by the teacher, should lead to many performances that are impressive because of their excellent contrasts.

Lesson Plan 9 • 25 minutes
February/March

Theme: *Simple, traditional dance steps and figures.*

Warm-up Activities
5 minutes

1 Skip by yourself to this lively country-dance music. Try to do the skipping step as I call out 'Skip, skip, skip, skip' so that we are all keeping in time with the music. Skip, skip, skip, skip; 5, 6, 7, 8.

2 This time, see if you have a different foot forward each time I call out 'Skip!' Skip, skip, skip, skip, change feet, change feet; one foot forward, the other foot; one foot forward, the other foot.

3 Keep skipping in time to the music, but listen to the drum beats. Two beats mean join hands and dance with a partner. One beat means separate and dance by yourself.

Teach Steps and Figures of the Lesson's Folk Dance
14 minutes

1 Stand next to a partner in our big circle, where you can all see me. Put your hands by your sides. I will come around and give you each a number – one or two.

2 Hands up the ones. Hands up the twos. Good. All correct.

3 Number ones, skip into the circle for four counts and clap your hands. Dance back out for four counts.

4 Number twos, do the same. Don't hurry. Take all four steps and clap hands on '4'. Use all four counts to come out again.

5 Face your partner. Give your partner one hand. Turn each other right around for four counts one way, then back with the other hand in the opposite direction for four counts.

6 Stand side by side, facing the way I am showing you (anti-clockwise). Give both hands to your partner and promenade around in our big circle for eight counts.

Dance — Circle Folk Dance
6 minutes

Music: Any lively, 32-bar English or Scottish dance tune.

Formation: A big circle, next to a partner, numbered one and two.

Bars 1–8 Ones dance to the centre, clapping hands on '4', and dance out again, back to places.

Bars 9–16 Twos dance into the centre, clapping hands on '4', and dance out again, back to places.

Bars 17–24 Partners face each other and turn, giving one arm for four, and turn back to places, giving other arm.

Bars 25–32 Partners all face anti-clockwise, and give both hands to each other to promenade around in the circle for eight counts.

Dance

Teaching notes and NC guidance
Development over 3 lessons

'Pupils should be taught to perform movements or patterns, including some from existing dance traditions and from different times and cultures.'

The folk-dance lesson often starts with pupils standing, clapping hands in time with the rhythmic beat of the music, and counting out the '1, 2, 3, 4, 5, 6, 7, 8' phrases of the music. Skipping, and trying to make each step on to your front foot hit the beat of the music, follows. Skipping is a '1, 2, 3' action, so a different foot should lead into each change of step, as we go 'Right, 2, 3; left, 2, 3; right, 2, 3; left, 2, 3; skip, 2, 3; skip, 2, 3.'

With young beginners in folk dance, a circle formation is the easiest to use. All can see and follow the teacher as he or she walks slowly through the figures of the typical four parts of the dance. We walk it through, then skip it through, then try it with the music, helped by the teacher's rhythmic accompaniment of the steps as a reminder and to ensure that each of the four parts of the dance receives its full eight counts. Four parts, each of eight bars of music, is a typical pattern for a folk dance, whether it is teacher-created, as this one is, or a traditional dance.

Warm-up Activities

1, 2 Most country-dance music is quite quick, at a speed that seems to fit the natural rhythm of most young pupils as they do their travelling. They easily fit their skipping into groups of eight counts, the phrasing of many 32-bar dances, with their 4×8 count patterns. The teacher will easily find one or more good demonstrators whose leading foot is changing each time, and use them to explain 'a different foot forward, each time.' 'Right foot forward; now left foot; right, 2, 3; left, 2, 3; change feet and change feet,' will soon have most of the class dancing in time with the music, and showing the ideal change of leading leg.

3 The varied ways to 'join hands' with a partner on two drum beats will include: nearer hands; left hands of both; right hands of both; both hands crossed in front; left hands low in front with right hands high above one partner's right shoulder. These can all be shown and/or taught.

Teach Steps and Figures of the Lesson's Folk Dance

1–4 A demonstration by the teacher will emphasise that four counts are taken for the slow skips into the centre. The hand-claps are done on the teacher's 'four!' Four counts are then taken to bring you back, slowly, to your own place in the circle.

5 The right-hands-joined turn is clockwise; the left-hands-joined turn is anti-clockwise, both turns using four counts of the music, so that no-one is early or late on count 'eight'.

6 Keeping the big circle round, and all couples keeping their distance from the couple in front of them, are emphasised in the eight-count promenade finish to the dance.

Circle Folk Dance

From performing the whole dance through, once only, accompanied by the teacher's reminder, pupils progress to dancing it continously, with less and less teacher involvement.

Lesson Plan 10 • 25 minutes
March

Theme: *Watching a moving object suggests ways of moving.*

Warm-up Activities
5 minutes

1   Balance on tiptoes, arms and legs straight, one foot in front of the other.

2   Stride out smartly, still with arms and legs straight, hurrying forwards, but looking up.

3   Push up high off one foot, reaching up with the opposite hand. Who can jump up the highest? Land with a nice, squashy landing on both feet and return to your starting, tiptoes position.

4   Ready. Balance on tiptoes; stride out firmly, with straight arms and legs; spring up from one foot and do your highest-ever jump.

Movement Skills Training
15 minutes

1   Listen to the words, and watch the bubbles being blown by several girls and boys. 'Floating calmly, gliding smoothly, soaring, sinking. Pop! All gone!'

2   Let's all say the words together as we watch other children make their bubbles fly. (Repeat words, very slowly, to accompany the several actions through to the end.)

3   We'll take each part separately and make neat actions as we think about how bubbles move. 'Floating calmly', silently on tiptoes, arms lifting you up, body turning, spinning, feeling no weight. Look at the way some bubbles are going up and down.

4   'Gliding smoothly', a little quicker, more streamlined in space. Straighten out and do big curves to turn. How will you hold your arms to help your smooth, gliding action?

5   In 'soaring' we start low and gradually increase speed to a higher level. Look up as you travel, reaching high and keeping your shape. Be streamlined and smooth. Down, down, up, up, up.

6   'Sinking' starts from a high position, gradually falling with no jerkiness, smoothly to the floor.

7   'Pop! All gone!' is the one quick movement. It could be a tiny jump; or arms and legs suddenly opening and closing quickly; or a drop down to a curled or stretched position on the floor.

Dance — Bubbles
5 minutes

1   Show me your still, lifted starting shape. I will say each set of words as your signal to show me how your bubble is moving. 'Floating calmly' – lifting, turning, gently along, up and down.

2   'Gliding smoothly' – a more streamlined, straighter pathway, arms in the glide, curving to turn.

3   'Soaring' – drop down low and travel straight, rising up on to tiptoes. A clear, streamlined body shape.

4   'Sinking' – from your highest balance, travel slowly along, dropping gradually. Smooth all the way.

5   'Pop! All gone!' – a quick move and be still. (Repeat. Improve the quality – how slow; how light; how gentle; how sudden? Perform.)

Dance

Teaching notes and NC guidance
Development over 2 lessons

'Pupils should be taught to use good posture and clear body shapes as they demonstrate good control, co-ordination, balance, poise, turning and stillness.'

It has been said that 'In Dance we move more fully than in everyday life', and in certain lessons the dancer is challenged to perform in a larger-than-life, semi-exaggerated manner, bringing every part of the body into the action.

Use of imagery once again gives the dancer a well-known, moving object to relate to. The dancer is not 'being' a bubble. He or she is moving, expressing the movement characteristics of the bubble, with its floating, hovering, lighter than air movements; its gentle, smooth, curving gliding; its streamlined soaring; and its soft, turning, falling to its sudden 'Pop! All gone!'

This slow dance is an excellent contrast to the usual high-speed movement of young pupils.

Representing the movement qualities of the slow, gentle object moving in space demands a well-controlled, balanced and poised use of the whole body.

Warm-up Activities

This four-part sequence with its controlled balance on tiptoes; its brisk striding with straight arms and legs; its vigorous upwards jump from one foot, reaching high with opposite hand; and its squashy, balanced landing into stillness on tiptoes, demands a strong, poised, whole-body control. In jumping, a well-bent knee reaching upwards is used in high jumps.

Movement Skills Training

Several containers of bubble-making soapy liquid, with the small rings through which the liquid is blown, are used by teacher and pupils at the start of the middle part of the lesson.

1, 2 The teacher says the words describing the bubbles' actions as they happen – floating, gliding, soaring, sinking. Different bubble-making pupils say the actions with the teacher.

3–7 Each of the five different bubble actions is now practised, felt, experienced by the class with the emphasis on the main quality of each movement: the weightless, calm floating; the streamlined, quicker, smooth gliding; the speeding up, soaring upwards; the gradual, smooth sinking; and the sudden, surprising 'Pop! All gone!' ending.

Bubbles Dance

1 Well practised, the class start, still and balanced, showing a shape that indicates the starting lifting, turning, gentle, buoyant, hither and thither, 'floating calmly'. The teacher's saying of the words produces the actions each time.

2 From the slow lifting and turning floaters, pupils change to a firmer, more direct and streamlined 'Gliding smoothly' with more travelling to all parts of the room.

3 After lowering to gain speed, their 'Soaring' is straight ahead, rising up on to tiptoes, still.

4 From their highest, still point of the soaring, they travel, 'Sinking', all the way to the floor.

5 After the slow, smooth sinking, the sudden, explosive 'Pop!' provides an exciting ending.

Lesson Plan 11 • 25 minutes
April

Theme: *Space, directions and levels.*

Warm-up Activities
5 minutes

1 Stand with your feet apart for balance, letting your fingers walk up to the space high above your head. Really stretch up, right up on to tiptoes.

2 Lower your straight arms down, feeling the space at your sides.

3 How far can you reach out in front of you with one hand? Bend your knees to help your balance. Now twist with the other hand to touch the space behind you.

4 Touch hips; touch knees; touch ankles; touch the floor. Coming back up, touch the floor again; toes; ankles; knees; and hips.

5 Can you remember your own space? I want you to travel to visit a side, an end, a corner, the middle, and then come back to your own space. Make your travelling so neat, quiet and interesting that I want to look at it. (Look out for walking, skipping, hopping, bouncing, floating, running, jumping, galloping, gliding, floating.)

Movement Skills Training
13 minutes

1 Watch these six travellers whose neat actions made me want to look at them. Thomas is tiptoeing quickly. Amy is bouncing with a twist. Rosie is leaping along with long arms and legs swinging. Adam is hopping, thrice on each foot. Meera is skipping with high knees and arms.

2 Try out some of those excellent actions to travel around. When I beat the tambourine and say 'Change!' can you be very clever and change to a new action, in a different direction, forwards, or sideways, or very carefully going backwards? Try to find out which actions are good for going sideways and backwards – and use your eyes to look for spaces. Go!

3 Let's travel with different body parts going first and leading us. Nose... one elbow... back... toes... seat... chest... side of one leg... knees. Did you see how often you changed direction?

Dance – Space Dance
7 minutes

1 Choose your own starting space, well away from all others. First with your hands by themselves, then with your feet by themselves, show me how you can reach to different levels to touch the spaces above, to the sides and behind you. A nice pattern would be 'Hands reach high; to the sides; behind; down low. One foot reaches forwards and to the side, the other reaches back and kicks up high.

2 Travel to visit a side, end, corner and the middle of the room. Try to use a variety of neat actions that take you in different directions with different body parts leading.

3 Find a partner and both stand, sharing the same space. To give our 'Space Dance' more variety we will have the number one partners staying in their spaces to start, while number twos travel away from and back to the shared space, after carefully dancing around all those working in their spaces. Partners then change places and actions.

4 Have another practice, then we will look at each half of the class in turn. Work hard to reach many spaces on the spot. Show me beautiful travelling actions in many directions.

5 Perform; comment; repeat; improve; perform again.

Dance

Teaching notes and NC guidance
Development over 3 lessons

'Pupils should be involved in the continuous process of planning, performing and evaluating, and the greatest emphasis should be on the actual performance.'

At the start of the lesson the teacher will put the class 'in the picture' regarding the lesson's theme. Such advance information is essential and fair, particularly if some form of assessment is being made of the created dance climax of the lesson.

The lesson's beginning, middle and end should all relate to, and lead up to, the creation of a dance. Only in this way can pupils know where they are; show, perform and feel; and understand and repeat.

Various ways to move to touch all of one's own personal space are identified, practised, commented on, and improved. Various ways to travel to a new space are encouraged by the teacher's commentary, praising good actions as they happen, and through neat demonstrations.

The challenge for partners to 'Plan a Space Dance, with one dancing on the spot and the other travelling to a space and back again, then both changing over their actions' is easy to respond to, because the lesson has led up to the creation of such a dance.

Warm-up Activities

1–3 An awareness of own personal space is developed by reaching high above head; wide to sides; to front and behind. High level above head, and medium level to front, side and to rear, are also being introduced and experienced.

4 Low-level awareness is taught through touching knees, toes and floor.

5 Travelling away from, and back to own exact spot on the floor, is more interesting and challenging when done to an eight-count rhythm set and chanted by the teacher.

Movement Skills Training

1 Praise, accompanied by a clear description of what is good, is always better than simply saying 'That's very good, Thomas,' because the nature of the goodness is shared with everyone.

2 This double meaning of 'Change!' is a challenging task, guaranteed to keep pupils' attention and inspire the forward planning that is needed to decide a new direction and a new action.

3 The 'body parts going first' inspires an immediate set of direction changes.

Space Dance

1 The 'Hands and feet to different levels' sequence will be impressive if, on a well-balanced, feet-wide-apart base, hands do three actions to all parts of the surrounding space bubble, followed by three balanced on one foot, where a foot reaches to other parts of the bubble.

2 Asking for 'Different parts leading' as pupils travel to all parts of the room, concentrates their thinking and focuses them on using many body parts as they keep changing direction.

3–5 One performing on the spot, while the partner travels and returns, is a good way to highlight and develop an awareness of space and levels.

Lesson Plan 12 • 25 minutes
May

Theme: *Spring and growth.*

Warm-up Activities
6 minutes

1 Stand with your feet wide apart and your upper body and arms hanging down. Slowly stretch up with arms reaching high and wide above your head. Drop arms back to your bent forward position.

2 Feel your body growing, then collapsing. Stretch high and wide, 2, 3. Arms and body drop, 2, 3. Keep practising.

3 Can you try the same actions from a tiny, curled-up, kneeling position? Now stretch back, shoulders and arms out wide. Can you feel your strong, firm stretch right through to your fingertips? Bend your arms, shoulders, and back to your curled-up, tiny finish.

4 Stand up and do three walking steps then a high jump, pushing straight up with both arms swinging high above your head. Step, step, step, spring high! Feel yourself growing very tall as you jump high in the air.

Movement Skills Training
7 minutes

1 Kneel down and curl to your smallest shape. Show me how you can start to grow, very slowly. Are you starting with your back, head, shoulders, elbows or arms? Show me clearly how you are rising to a full, wide stretch position.

2 Gently, return to your curled-up starting position and practise growing, very slowly, once again.

3 Are you rising straight up, or with a little twist from side to side? Maybe one shoulder, elbow or hand leads, then the other in an interesting, twisting way to rise and grow.

Dance — Spring Dance
12 minutes

1 Find a partner and both kneel down near each other for the first part of our 'Spring Dance' – the flower seed growing. Curl up small, close to the floor.

2 Slowly, start to grow and show me which parts of you are leading as you rise to your full, wide flower shape. You might even twist your full flower shape to look at the sun. (Teacher, moving slowly, can represent the sun as a focus.)

3 Let's have a look at our partner's way of rising, growing and stretching out towards the sunshine. Decide who is going first.

4 Now the other partner. Can you surprise your partner and me by making a sudden stretch into your final stretch shape? Begin.

5 Well done, everyone. I saw lots of beautiful growing actions and flower shapes. Can the first partner stand now for the second part of our dance – mother bird and baby bird. Mother bird flies around the nest, looking for food for the kneeling baby bird in the nest, reaching and stretching up to receive the food brought by the mother, who then flies off again. Practise your flying, collecting food, and your reaching up and receiving the food.

6 Mother bird now thinks that the baby is old enough to rise up and fly away from the nest. Mother signals 'Come on, follow me' and the baby slowly rises, tries out its wings, and follows the mother, occasionally stumbling, falling and getting up again.

7 That was really good, mothers and babies. Let's practise the whole dance from the beginning, then look at lots of couples.

Dance

Teaching notes and NC guidance
Development over 3 lessons

'Pupils should be able to show that they can improve performance, through practice, alone and with a partner'

Prior to an improved performance, there must be:

a a clear understanding of the specific nature of the lesson's theme. Vague descriptions such as 'We are exploring stretching and curling' or 'We are making shapes' are abstract and difficult to understand. They do not conjure up an easily visualised, clearly understood image. 'Our lesson is about the way that plants and birds start to grow in spring' will capture pupils' interest and tell them where the lesson is going.

b opportunities to be taught, experience, practise, repeat and be questioned about what we mean by growing actions, generally from a curled-up starting shape.

c discussion and practice of the more specific actions of a seed slowly growing and rising to a full flower shape, or a baby bird rising slowly, trying out its wings, and making its first stumbling attempts at flying.

d a definite, clearly understood structure to the eventual dance, decided by the teacher. All vagueness is removed by the clear form of the dance: partners, near each other, both perform the seed growing at the start; one partner then stands to represent the mother bird looking for, then offering food to the baby bird in the nest; the mother bird signals to the baby to try to rise up and fly away from the nest; the baby is unsteady to start with, but eventually manages the action.

Warm-up Activities

1, 2 From a feet-wide-apart base, with the upper body hanging down, pupils slowly reach up to an arms-wide-stretched position, using every joint in the body to make it grow.

3 From a tiny, curled, kneeling start, they stretch again until all upper-body, shoulder and arm joints are fully stretched, making the body grow once more.

4 The stretch to being as tall as possible is now practised after a short walk into a vigorous upwards jump, accompanied by arms swinging up high.

Movement Skills Training

Shared choice teaching, where the teacher decides the nature of the activity and the class decide the actions ('Show me how you can start to grow, very slowly') produces a wide variety of results. To help develop pupils' decision-making, the teacher reminds them of body parts that can lead from curled small to a full-grown stretch.'Body-parts awareness' can refer to the order of smooth unrolling by the various joints, or the unusual twisting/rising growth.

Spring Dance

1, 2 Adjacent partners start to grow like flower seeds to their full, wide, stretched shape. They concentrate on showing the teacher, as requested, 'which parts of you are leading'.

3, 4 While one partner is observing the other partner, he or she might decide to show a contrasting growth action and finish for variety. Number one's smooth, joint-by-joint, straight unfurling of the upper body might lead to number two showing a twisting, turning, rotating, looking-for-the-sun growth.

5–7 The seed growing and the baby bird feeding and then flying off are images that help to inspire easily understood situations and actions. Good images 'stir the imagination' and speed up the lesson's progress. 'Like a baby bird trying out its wings' is very easy to understand, picture, and to try to represent. Both these partner work examples, the seed and the mother and baby bird, also provide the observers with performances that they can easily relate to, comment on, and learn from.

Lesson Plan 13 • 25 minutes
June

Theme: *Feelings.*

Warm-up Activities
5 minutes

Help me, please, by saying the words and doing the actions, as we do our lively walking or skipping around together:

If you're happy and you know it, clap your hands,
If you're happy and you know it, clap your hands,
If you're happy and you know it, and you really want to
  show it,
If you're happy and you know it, clap your hands.

If you're happy and you know it, smile and wave,
... twist and shake... jump for joy...

Movement Skills Training
13 minutes

1 Without travelling from where you are now, show me a happy face. Show me a whole-body shape that tells me you are happy.

2 Show me an angry face... angry hands... angry whole body.

3 Well done. You are using your body and parts of your body to show me feelings. Now show me a proud body with its proud back, head, arms – very pleased with yourself.

4 Now you are frightened. Show it in your face and your whole body, hiding, shrinking away from something unpleasant.

5 Well done. All those feelings were shown on the spot. Can you try to use body activities to show me your feelings now? How about dancing around, happily waving your hands?

6 Still travelling, show me angry feet stamping the floor and angry hands punching the air.

7 Clever boys and girls, let me see your swaggering, very proud walking, like someone very important. Look at me! I'm the best!

8 Fear now, as you rush away, stop to look back, hide away from that terrible something behind you, following you. You might even have to crouch down low, as you hide from it.

Dance — Feelings
7 minutes

1 Find a partner and decide which of your feelings you want to use for our partners dance. Happy? Angry? Proud? Frightened?

2 Practise on the spot by yourself. Try to make a little pattern that you can remember and repeat, as you show me your own ways of moving to show your feelings. If I watch you, will I see a repeating pattern? (Encourage three or four parts to the short sequence on the spot, e.g. angry stamping, punching, jumping.)

3 Our dance will end with both of you dancing together. Decide which actions you will use. Will you skip and clap happily; stamp and punch angrily; swagger and step high proudly; or creep and hide, very frightened? Please decide and practise.

4 Before we practise the whole dance through, decide on your final shape and position.   .

5 Show me your starting shape and position. My signals will be a drum beat for number one to start; a drum beat for number two to start; then a drum beat for your final part, together.

6 Once more through, then we will share some of these brilliant ideas for showing feelings.

Dance

Teaching notes and NC guidance
Development over 4 lessons

'Pupils should be taught to explore moods and feelings and express and communicate ideas.'

Expressing feelings through Dance movement, rather than through speech or facial (acting) contortions, is not easy. The lesson's pattern and structure is designed to lead the class, bit by bit, through to the creation of the dance climax. After the easy 'Follow the Teacher' opening song, expressing happiness through actions, the middle part of the lesson, with a lot of direct teaching, challenges the class to indulge whole-heartedly in big body movements to express happiness, anger, pride and fear, both in one's own space and while travelling.

Good examples will have been shared with the class who now understand that it is important to plan a movement expression. The teacher's own repertoire will also have helped. The dance climax challenge is specific and therefore easily understood. The request to 'make a little pattern that you can remember and repeat' is in line with the joined-up actions they have always been taught to use in their Dance lessons.

The eventual dance will be unique with each one of the pair doing their own different dance, then combining to respond to each other in a third dance. 'Sharing some of these brilliant ideas for showing feelings' through movement will therefore be an essential part of the lesson structure.

Warm-up Activities

Straight away, pupils are singing and thinking about ways to behave when happy, and how to express these feelings through movement.

Movement Skills Training

1–4 The enthusiastic teacher-leader will lead by example and point out the many good examples seen in the class. He or she will emphasise 'Come on. Let our expressions be larger than life so that someone, from a distance, could easily recognise them.' He or she will also remind them, 'No speaking. Let your actions and your gestures, only, tell me what you are feeling.'

5–8 With lots of suggestions and examples from the teacher and selected pupils, the showing of feelings on the move can provide an exciting, expression-filled hall. The challenge for the teacher is to see, and share the many excellent performances with the class.

Feelings Dance

1 Partners are asked to agree and choose one feeling only for their individual and shared dance.

2 Within the 'little pattern' requested by the teacher, actions on the spot and actions on the move around the room are encouraged to provide attractive contrast and variety. Each of the three or four parts of the sequence should last only a few seconds.

3–6 Joint planning by the partners decides the actions for the final part of the dance – knowing that there will be demonstrations by everyone to look forward to and prepare for. Each partner dances alone, one after the other, to drum beat signals from the teacher, then both dance their combined presentation. Observers, later, are asked 'Please watch and tell me what you particularly liked about any of the dancing couples' whole dance.'

Year 1

Lesson Plan 14 • 25 minutes
July

Theme: *Vocal sounds as movement accompaniment and inspiration.*

Warm-up Activities
5 minutes

1 Listen to the rhythm of the lively music as you walk, skip, run, bounce or run and jump. When I sound the tambourine twice, find a partner and dance together. You can be joined or separate. Go!

2 When the tambourine sounds once, separate and dance by yourself.

3 When the tambourine sounds twice, find a partner, different from the one you had last time, and dance together.

Movement Skills Training
10 minutes

1 I am going to sing out some of the actions we have performed in our Dance lessons. Listen very carefully and see if you can keep going with my words. Some of the words might be stretched out and others might be shortened. Are you ready?

2 W-a-l-k; be still; f-l-o-p; stretch; s-k-i-p; stamp; t-u-r-n; clap; c-u-r-l; balance. Well done. You kept up with me splendidly.

3 We can also move to other words that aren't movement words. Try moving to 'Tick tock' just where you are. Say it and do it for me. Tick, tock, tick, tock, light and quick.

4 Show me how you can travel to a wind-blowing sound – whoosh!

5 Can you be brilliant and invent a sound or two sounds I have never heard before, and show me how you can move to them? Join the sounds and the movements exactly together.

6 Make your movements and your shapes very neat and let me hear your invented sounds loud and clear.

Dance — Voice Sounds
10 minutes

1 You have been making your own sounds to accompany your varied movements. Can you think of anything you might be doing, or any place where you might be going during the holidays, that might help us to make our last dance together for this school year? Suggest some of the action words that might be used to accompany a short dance if we stretch out or shorten parts of the word. Swimming... paddling... flying... driving... shopping... painting.

2 Can anyone tell me a place where you might be going that is an interesting word to dance to? Florida... Glasgow... Majorca... Bournemouth... Vancouver... Scotland.

3 Decide your action word or a place, and then practise your short dance, saying the word and trying to include some stillness, travelling, a jump, and maybe a turn or a rise and fall.

4 Take a deep breath before you start so that you can make one or more parts of the word s-t-r-e-e-t-ch out and be interesting to listen to and watch.

5 Finish your little dance, beautifully still and with a shape that makes me want to look at you.

6 Well done everyone. I see lots of good action and I hear lots of interesting voice sounds. Let's have each half of the class in turn looking at and commenting on the other half.

7 When you are watching, look out for and tell me about good actions, good shapes and excellent use of the voice that made the word good for movement.

Dance

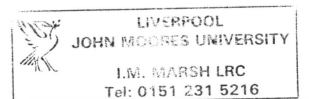

LIVERPOOL
JOHN MOORES UNIVERSITY

I.M. MARSH LRC
Tel: 0151 231 5216

Teaching notes and NC guidance
Development over 3 lessons

'Pupils should be able to show that they can: (a) plan and perform simple skills safely; (b) show control in linking actions together.'

In the lively warm-up travelling start to the lesson, there will be much revision of the many and varied travelling actions, and requests from the teacher for neat, quiet, controlled footwork often illustrated by a quick demonstration. There will also be the request for safe travelling, always looking for 'good spaces, visiting all parts of the room – the sides, ends, corners as well as the middle, and never following anyone.'

In addition to practising safely and well, the skills of travelling are practised rhythmically to the accompanying music. The teacher's voice is the rhythmic accompaniment to the idea of stretching and shortening well-known actions in the middle part of the lesson. Pupils are then challenged to invent a sound and plan how to move to it, showing clear shapes and neat movement.

In the created dance climax of the lesson, pupils start off with an action or place word, and then have to plan a pattern of varied speed actions, trying to include 'some stillness, travelling, a jump and maybe a turn or rise and fall'. This is a double challenge, namely to link several actions smoothly and to include interesting and possibly exciting changes of speed.

Warm-up Activities

Attentiveness and immediate responses, always important at the start of the lesson, are ensured because pupils have to listen for the teacher's signals to change to and from partner work. Good examples of 'dancing together' need to be shown. (One or both hands joined; elbows linked; hand on shoulder; both hands forwards, down low, or high between.)

Movement Skills Training

1–2 Some action words can have a long, drawn-out response, such as turning, bending, stretching, curling, sliding. Other words can have a sudden response, such as jump, reach, explode. The teacher mixes the sudden and the lingering, for variety.

3 'Tick tock' for a side to side, pendulum sway; 'Boomp boomp' for bounces, for example.

4 The 'Whoosh!' of the firework rocket up into space was first met the previous November. The more prolonged, wind-blowing sound 'Whoosh!' is an equally good image.

5–6 Planning to invent a completely new sound and its accompanying action is a difficult challenge. The teacher needs to be aware of good work to show as helpful examples.

Voice Sounds Dance

Pupils now have to decide to use a holiday activity or place name as the vocal accompaniment to their dance, and then 'show control in linking actions together' by using some or all of the teacher's suggested 'travelling, jump, turn, rise or fall' and 'beautifully still finish with shape that makes me want to look at you.' A mixture of high-quality actions, beautiful shapes and excellent use of the voice can bring the year's programme to a most satisfactory and enjoyable end.

Games

Introduction to Games

Individual and team games are part of our national heritage and an essential part of the Physical Education programme. Skills learned during Games lessons easily lend themselves to being practised away from school, alone or with friends or parents, and are the skills most likely to be used in participating in worthwhile physical and sociable activities long after leaving school – an important, long-term aim in Physical Education.

Vigorous, whole-body activity in the fresh air promotes normal, healthy growth and physical development, stimulating the heart, lungs and big muscle groups, particularly the legs.

Games lessons come nearest of all Physical Education activities to demonstrating what we understand by the expression 'children at play'. Pupils are involved in play-like, exciting, adventurous chasing and dodging as they try to outwit opponents in games and competitive activities. Such close, friendly 'combat' with and against others can help to compensate for the increasingly isolated, over-protected, self-absorbed nature of much of today's childhood, with little healthy adventure.

Games are taught outdoors, in the fresh air, in the playground. For infant classes, the playground 'classroom' can be a netball court, if the school has one, or a rectangle, sub-divided into six or eight 8–10-metre rectangles.

The lesson starts with warming-up and footwork activities to improve stopping, starting, dodging, marking, running and jumping. Skills are taught individually and in pairs in the middle part of the lesson. During the course of a year a wide variety of games equipment will be experienced, ideally with the same equipment being used by all in the same lesson, so that teaching applies to all. In the most important, final part of the lesson, three different group practices or games provide an exciting and varied climax with near-continuous action for all.

The following monthly lesson plans and accompanying notes aim to provide teachers and schools with a wide variety of material for lesson content, development and progression. Each lesson is repeated three or four times to allow plenty of time for planning, practising and improving, which are essential elements in good practice in the National Curriculum.

The playground Games 'classroom'

Infant-school Games lessons should be taught out of doors on the playground. Where no netball court is marked, the 'classroom' is a painted rectangle of six to eight 8–10-metre square grids.

This painted rectangle is essential because it:

a contains the class in a limited space within which the teacher can see, manage and be easily seen and heard by the whole class, not needing to raise and strain his or her voice by shouting to be heard over great distances

b gives the spaces needed for the three activities of the final group practices part of the lesson. Each space is normally two adjacent rectangles across the court. Where there are eight grids or small rectangles, two pairs can be used for any activity that benefits from extra space, such as short tennis

c prevents accidents by keeping the class well away from any potential hazards such as concrete seats, hutted classrooms, fences or walls, all of which should be several metres outside the games rectangle

d provides lines which are used in hundreds of ways during the infant years' Games programme. Pupils run and jump over; balance on; can be 'safe' on in chasing games; aim at; play net games over; use in limited-area 'invent a game or practice' situations; play end-to-end, two-with or two-against games; do side-to-side sprint relays.

With a new class each September, the teacher's main emphasis during a Games lesson on the playground is training the class to be aware of, and to remain within, the outside lines of the 'playground classroom' rectangle. 'Show me your best running as you go to all parts of our playground classroom. Visit the ends, sides, the middle and always keep inside the lines of our pretend classroom.'

Games equipment

Teachers should ensure they have the following:

○ sets of 30 of: small balls; medium balls; large balls; beanbags; skipping ropes; playbats; hoops; short tennis rackets

○ 10 × long, 24 ft (7 metre) skipping ropes for group skipping and for use as 'nets' for tennis and quoits

○ 10 × rubber quoits

○ 6 × 8 in (20 cm) foam balls

- ❍ playground chalk
- ❍ 1 × set Kwik Cricket
- ❍ 8 × marker cones.

Safe teaching of Games

A teacher's checklist of *safe practices* will include:

- ❍ sensible, safe clothing with no watches, jewellery, rings, long trousers that catch heels or unbunched hair that impedes vision
- ❍ good supervision by the teacher whose circulation, mainly on the outside looking in, means that the majority of the class can be seen at all times, with few behind the teacher's back
- ❍ fast-moving, dodging and chasing children must be trained to remain inside the lines of the games rectangle
- ❍ good behaviour with a tradition of quiet tongues and feet, and instant responses to instructions
- ❍ an awareness by the class of danger points such as fences, walls, sheds, seats, or steps into buildings if a pupil has to leave the 'playground classroom' to recover a wandering ball
- ❍ good teaching, which aims to develop skilful, well-controlled, safe movement, is a major contributor to safe practice
- ❍ if there is strong sunshine, the teacher should face the sun when teaching or introducing a new activity, or when presenting a demonstration. The class will have the sun behind them, enabling them to see and understand more easily.

Essential traditions, when teaching, include:

1. Insisting on a safe, unselfish sharing of space; immediate responses to instructions, particularly the one to 'Stop!'; and a quiet atmosphere with pupils keen to improve. The class should understand they must be 'found working, not waiting' as their contribution to almost non-stop activity.

2. Inaction and 'lesson dead spots' must be avoided. These are caused by over-long explanations; too many stoppages for demonstrations followed by lengthy comments and discussion; and poor responses from a class who need to be asked to 'Stop!' too often.

3. While the thinking and planning, reflecting and evaluating requirements of the NC should always be a concern in teaching PE, the main emphasis must always be on the doing, the performing, the action.

4. The teacher's main aim should be a flowing, almost non-stop lesson with optimum activity. Children enjoy a lesson when 'it is fun; is exciting; has lots of action; all have a turn; you learn interesting new things; it makes you fitter; rules make it fair for everyone.'

Planned aims, as in all areas of Physical Education, include:

1. The promotion of normal, healthy growth and physical development.

2. The learning of skills to develop neat, skilful, well-controlled, versatile movement.

3. Helping pupils become good learners as well as good movers. Pupils are challenged to think for themselves and make decisions about their actions.

4. Developing pupils' self-confidence and self-esteem as achievements are recognised, praised and shared with others.

5. Developing desirable social qualities through friendly, co-operative, close relationships, which are an ever-present feature of these lessons.

6. Satisfying every pupil's entitlement to achieve physical competence in a broad and balanced Physical Education programme.

How to teach a Games skill or practice

Excellent lesson 'pace' is expressed in almost non-stop activity with no bad behaviour stoppages and no 'dead spots' caused by long queues, over-long explanations or too many time-consuming demonstrations. The teaching of each of the skills which combine to make a Games lesson determines the quality of the lesson's pace – a main feature of an excellent Physical Education lesson.

A typical Games lesson, with its warm-up and footwork practices, skills practices and small-sided group practices and games, will include about a dozen skills. Whatever the skill, there is a pattern for teaching it:

1   **Quickly into action**. In a few words, explain the task and challenge the class to start. 'Can you stand, two big steps apart, and throw the small ball to your partner for a two-handed catch?' If a short demonstration is needed, then the teacher can work with a pupil who has been alerted. Class practice should start quickly after the five seconds it took the teacher to make the challenge.

2   **Emphasise the main teaching points, one at a time, while the class is working.** A well-behaved class does not need to be stopped to listen to the next point. 'Hold your hands forwards to show your partner where to aim'; 'Watch the ball into your cupped hands.'

3   **Identify and praise good work, while class is working.** Comments are heard by all; remind the class of key points; and inspire the praised to even greater effort. 'Well done, Sarah and Daniel. You are throwing and catching at the right height and speed, and watching the ball into your hands.'

4   **Teach for individual improvement while class is working.** 'Patrick, hold both hands forward to give Christine a still target to aim at'; 'Ann and Alan, stand closer. You are far too far apart.'

5   **A demonstration** can be used, briefly, to show good quality or an example of what is required. 'Stop, everyone, please, and watch how Cara and Michael let their hands "give" as they receive the ball, to stop it bouncing out again.'

6   **Very occasionally (once, or twice at most in a lesson to avoid taking too much activity time) a short demonstration can be followed by comments.** 'Stop and watch Leroy and Emily. Tell me what makes their throwing and catching so smooth and accurate.' The class watch about six throws and three or four comments are invited. For example, 'They are nicely balanced with one foot forward', 'Their hands are well forward, to take the ball early, then give, smoothly and gently.'

7   **Thanks are given to performers and those making helpful comments.** Further practice takes place with reminders of the good things seen and commented on. We remember what we see and pupils need to be given the opportunity to try some of the things seen and praised.

National Curriculum requirements for Games –
Key Stage 1: the main features

'The Government believes that two hours of physical activity a week, including the National Curriculum for Physical Education and extra-curricular activities, should be an aspiration for all schools. This applies to all key stages.'

Programme of Study

Pupils should be taught to:

a travel with, send and receive a ball and other equipment in different ways. Equipment used in the following lessons includes balls of various sizes and textures, bats, rackets, beanbags, quoits, skipping ropes of different lengths, and hoops

b develop these skills for simple net, striking/fielding and invasion-type games. Neat, controlled footwork with changes of speed and direction used to pursue, dodge or simply to give you ample practising room, makes chasing games more exciting and safe

c play simple, competitive net, striking/fielding and invasion-type games that they and others have made, using simple tactics for attacking and defending. From the simplest 'Can you aim at the line between you and your partner and count your good hits to see who is the winner?' to 'Can you invent a simple, 1-against-1 game, using one ball and a part of a line, and using the skills we have just practised?' to 'Can your group of four make up a game, using the large ball and two of the lines around the area?'

At every stage, the pupils will be asked to consider, 'How will you score in your little game? What will be the main rule to make your game fair for everyone? How will your game re-start after a score? Can you think of any extra ways to make the game more exciting?' and, if necessary, 'How can we help to make scoring easier?' (e.g. defending team will be 'passive', not going for the ball).

Attainment Target

Pupils should be able to demonstrate that they can:

a select and use skills, actions and ideas appropriately, applying them with co-ordination and control (e.g. throw ball up, jump to catch it, land nicely poised)

b vary, copy, repeat and link skills, actions and ideas in ways that suit the activities (i.e. ample equipment needed to provide an implement each to enable such practising)

c talk about differences between own and others' work and suggest ways to improve their own performance

d recognise and describe the changes that happen to the body during exercise (from increased warmth, perspiration, deep breathing, chest rising and falling, and fatigue, to 'feeling relaxed, calm, happy, good inside, proud, excited').

Main NC Headings when considering assessment, progression and expectation

○ **Planning** – in a safe, thoughtful, focused way, thinking ahead to an intended outcome. The set criteria are used and there is evidence of originality and variety

○ **Performing and improving performance** – pupils work hard, concentrating on the main feature of the task, to present a neat, efficient, poised, confident performance, under control

○ **Linking actions** – pupils work harder for longer, smoothly and safely, using space sensibly, and are able to remember and repeat the whole sequence successfully from its start right through to its controlled finish

○ **Reflecting and making judgements** to help pupils progress and improve, as they plan again adapting and altering as required, guided by their own and others' comments and judgements.

Year 1 Games programme

Pupils should be able to:

Autumn	Spring	Summer
1 Respond readily and safely to instructions.	**1** Show improved body management in many skills, and display increasing self-confidence.	**1** Practise running for quality and variety with speed and direction changes, always conscious of good sharing of space.
2 Contribute to class tradition of quiet, almost non-stop work, listening to the teacher.	**2** Keep practising to improve and remember simple skills.	**2** Run and jump long and high to experience different actions, take-offs and landings.
3 Run and jump with vigour, good spacing, and lifting of heels, knees, arms and chest.	**3** Use varied implements in a variety of ways – ball, rope, hoop, quoit, beanbag, bat.	**3** Enjoy safe, enthusiastic chasing and dodging games.
4 Practise with wide range of implements – rope, ball, hoop, beanbag, quoit, playbat.	**4** Be keen on dodging and chasing games, using good footwork, with speed and direction changes.	**4** Show more confidence in using games implements – bat and ball, beanbag, rope, quoit, hoop, ball.
5 Practise many ways to send and control a ball – throw, strike, kick, head, gather, carry.	**5** Practise skills with a partner with increasing control and understanding, trying to please.	**5** Be physically active with good attitude to exercise in fresh air. 'It's good for you, makes you fit and it's good fun.'
6 Experience pleasure and excitement through achievement.	**6** Perform linked movements – run and jump; throw, run, catch.	**6** Show increased control in sending, receiving and travelling with a ball alone, and with a partner.
7 Practise with a rope to jump over, balance along, and learn to skip.	**7** Respond well to praise and encouragement.	**7** Practise bat and ball skills carefully, adapting to learn from experience alone, and with a partner.
8 Plan to respond to challenge – 'Can you...?'	**8** Learn to skip in a variety of ways to keep warm in winter.	**8** Skip in many ways, on the spot and travelling in many directions.
9 Aim beanbag at hoop on ground or held high by partner.	**9** Invent a simple game with a partner, to use, for example, a ball, a line and a hoop. Agree the main rule and how to score.	**9** Show improved hand and eye co-ordination with a partner, throwing quoit or beanbag over a net.
10 Perform vigorously to become and stay warm in cold weather.	**10** Play a simple 2 v 2 game in a small area. Decide main rules and how to score and re-start.	**10** Link movements smoothly: Skip on spot and moving; bat down for 3, bat up for 3.
11 Co-operate with partner in leading and following, and in showing favourite activities.	**11** Watch less skilful 'learners' demonstrating and encourage them.	**11** Describe what was done and how it was done. Identify the quality admired.
12 Send a big ball to partner for an easy catch, trying out a variety of ways.	**12** Be able and willing to use good points seen and discussed during demonstrations.	**12** Make up and play simple games with a partner and 2 v 2, agreeing scoring system, main rules and how to re-start.
13 Demonstrate with enthusiasm.		
14 Observe demonstrations. Point out features that are worth copying.		

Lesson Plan 1 • 30 minutes
September

Emphasis on: *(a) establishing a tradition of almost non-stop, whole-hearted and enthusiastic participation; supported by (b) instant responses to instructions and signals; and (c) experiencing pleasure through participation in activity.*

Warm-up and Footwork Practices
4 minutes

1   Good running is quiet and you don't follow anyone. Show me your best running with a good lifting of heels, knees, arms and chest.

2   Run straight, not curving, and try to visit every part of our playgound 'classroom'. (Primary school children will all run in an anti-clockwise circle, unless taught not to do so.)

3   When I call 'Stop!', be in a space all by yourself, standing perfectly still. Stop! (Demand the immediate response that this activity is designed for.)

Skills Practices: with small bats and balls
10 minutes

Individual practices

1   Can you balance your ball on the bat? Now can you bat the ball upwards very gently?

2   Try walking slowly forwards, alternately balancing and hitting the ball a little way upwards.

3   Bat the ball up and in front of you, let it bounce up, then bat it up again. Be very gentle, using your wrist to move the bat, not elbow or shoulder. What is your best score?

Partner practices

1   One using the bat, one using a hand, can you keep the ball going up and down with one bounce on the ground in between? What is your best score, non-stop? Let other partner try with the bat.

2   One with bat strikes ball carefully for partner to catch. Ball can be dropped, then hit, or hit from hand. Stand only 3 metres apart with catcher's hands reaching well forwards as a target.

Group Practices
16 minutes

Small bat and ball each

Practise freely, on the spot and moving. A little sequence, standing then moving, would be interesting (e.g. bat up, standing, bat down, walking).

Partners with a beanbag

2–3 metres apart, throw and catch, low (below knees), medium (to chest), higher (just above head). Throw with one hand, catch with two.

Hoop each

Show me ways to use the hoop, sometimes on the ground, sometimes in one or both hands (e.g. balancing round, on ground, and bowl or skip in hand or hands).

Games

Teaching notes and NC guidance
Development over 4 lessons

Warm-up and Footwork Practices

1 Running may be a completely natural activity but it will be done very badly unless good practice is explained and insisted upon. Noisy, flat-footed clumping around is often seen and a silent demonstration by the teacher or a small group of pupils will have an immediate effect, particularly if the teacher says 'I am going to close my eyes while you are practising. I do not want to hear a sound.'

2 All primary school children run in an anti-clockwise circle, all following one another, unless taught to 'Run on straight lines, never following anyone. Visit all parts of the space, the ends, the sides, the middle, the corners, never curving.'

3 The command to be standing, still, in a space, well away from all others, is an exercise in responding to a signal (immediately!) and in thinking about own and others' space.

Skills Practices: with small bats and balls

Individual practices

1 Because of traditional good weather in September, we can have a bat and ball lesson. Batting skills are difficult and tend to be rather static, so they are done in warmer weather. To help with the balancing and hitting, the children are asked to hold their bat or racket near the head, not at the end of the handle.

2 With a bent arm, pupils will have greater control and can hold the bat near to them, where their eyes can see the ball well, just in front of their faces.

3 The hit up is high enough to let the ball bounce on the ground and come up to waist height for the next strike. The movement takes place in the wrist, not the elbow or shoulder.

Partner practices

1 Partners stand close enough to touch each other. The practice starts with the ball being dropped between them on to the ground by one partner. The other partner hits under the ball to strike it vertically upwards to bounce for the next hit by the other partner. Good footwork takes the player to the correct spot each time.

2 Batter chooses to hit from the hand as in table tennis or to drop for a bounce up for the hit. Catcher's outstretched hands show the batter where to aim.

Group practices

Small bat and ball each

Free practice allows a reinforcement of some of the difficult skills of balancing, striking and judging force. Alternating on-the-spot with on-the-move practices leads to interesting and challenging sequences and linking skills together.

Partners with a beanbag

Sending and receiving are easily and pleasantly practised with a beanbag, which is easy to grab and does not bounce away.

Hoop each

The hoop can be on the ground for jumps and balances, and in the hands for skipping, spinning and bowling.

Lesson Plan 2 • 30 minutes
October

Emphasis on: *(a) continuing to establish the habit of practising quietly and listening to the teacher while practising; (b) good sharing of space and awareness of others for safe, satisfactory and enjoyable practice.*

Warm-up and Footwork Practices
4 minutes

1   Can you run, looking for spaces to run through?

2   Run very slowly, or even on the spot, if you are near others. Go faster when you see a big space.

3   When I call 'Stop!' show me how quickly you can run and jump to land and stand, perfectly still on tiptoes, on one of the lines.

Skills practices: with hoops
10 minutes

Individual practices

1   Put your hoop on the ground, nicely spaced away from others. Now run and jump in and out of all the hoops, without touching them, like stepping stones.

2   Can you run and jump high and do a nice, squashy landing into any empty hoop? Are you jumping up with one or both feet?

3   Now lift up a hoop and practise freely using one or both hands (e.g. bowling, spinning, skipping, throwing and catching).

Partner practices

1   Partner tag, where the chaser may only touch their partner when the partner is not 'safe' in a hoop.

2   Now show your partner something you enjoy doing with your hoop. Then your partner will show you something else, and you might learn a new skill. You might even be able to perform it at the same time.

Group Practices
16 minutes

Large ball each

Practise throwing and catching on the move. Can you throw low (waist), medium (chest) and high (above head)? Use two hands for throw and catch. Watch ball all the way into your reaching, cupped hands.

Partners: with a hoop

Can you and your partner invent an activity where you can mirror each other in some way? For example, one each side, bowling one hoop; walking sideways inside own hoop, holding it in two hands; both bowl to each other at same time from 2 metres.

3 Skipping rope each

Practise freely, but try some on the spot and some on the move. Can you do a double beat of your feet for each turn of the rope? Can you go forwards, running one foot after the other?

Games

Teaching notes and NC guidance
Development over 4 lessons

Warm-up and Footwork Practices

1 Good sharing of space reduces accidents and frustration and lets you practise in a satisfactory way. Such sharing is safe and sociable.

2 We have to learn to adjust to the space available, slowing down when near others and speeding up when there is lots of room.

3 The signal to 'Stop!' and then run and jump to land on the nearest line, perfectly still on tiptoes, is an exercise in being attentive and responding immediately to instructions.

Skills Practices: with hoops

Individual practices

1 The 25–30 hoops of a typical class are spaced out to create sets of 'stepping stones', with some close enough together for a series of steps and others spread wide for running and jumping.

2 Try one- and two-footed take-offs as you jump up high to land with a 'squashy' action and a 'give' in the knees. The landing can be with both feet or with one foot, then the other.

3 Free, but guided practice, with hoop in hand or hands encourages a variety of class responses including the quite easy spinning on the ground, wrist, ankle or waist; the quite difficult bowling and walking beside the hoop; and the very difficult skipping, either low from side to side, or overhead.

Partner practices

1 With lots of hoops to 'hide' in as safe havens, dodging partners have to be encouraged to be 'good sports' and not linger too long in the hoop. When caught, the dodger becomes the chaser.

2 It is hoped that the watching partner will say something complimentary to the partner who has just demonstrated a favourite activity. It is also hoped that many of the watchers will learn something new to try.

Group Practices

Large ball each

Habitual practising 'on the move' becomes important from now on as the weather starts to become colder. Throwing to oneself on the move, using both hands, is best done throwing straight upwards. The challenge to throw to different heights gives practice in 'feeling' how much effort to put into a variety of throws. Receiving is as important as the sending and a good hand position, cupped with fingers spread forwards, is needed.

Partners: with a hoop

To plan or 'invent' a game or a practice is an important element of the NC, as are the performing and the reflecting/evaluating. This sociable and creative activity brings great pleasure to the participants, and can add something new to the class repertoire.

Skipping rope each

Most Year 1 children are able to learn how to skip if given enough opportunities. A long, slow overhead pull to make the rope slide towards you for a step over, is stage one. Hands are wide and the turn of the rope is made with a small wrist action.

Lesson Plan 3 • 30 minutes
November

Emphasis on: *(a) the pleasure of working with a partner; (b) the good feeling when your improvement and achievement are recognised, praised and used to help others to improve as well.*

Warm-up and Footwork Practices
5 minutes

1 Play follow the leader with a partner where the leader does a short, easy-to-copy walk, then run, then jump. Is there something special about the walk (e.g. straight legs), the run (e.g. with high knee raising), the jump (e.g. with a half turn to finish)?

2 Five points tag. All have five points to start with. Each time you are caught by someone touching you, you lose a point. (No dangerous pushing – touch gently.)

Skills Practices: with beanbags
10 minutes

Individual practices

1 Walk forwards, throwing up, clapping hands, then catching. The hand-clap puts your hands in a good position for a catch, cupped and high in front of your eyes.

2 Throw up, not very high, and catch (about head height). Throw up higher and catch (just above head height). Now throw up as high as you think you can catch. If you can do all that on the move, that will be excellent.

Partner practices

1 Stand close and try underarm throwing with one hand, catching with two hands. Catcher, hold your hands forwards and cupped where you want your partner to aim. Thrower, swing forwards, back and then throw with a long arm swing.

2 Can you walk or jog, side by side, and gently throw the beanbag to your partner, just in front of him or her, and high enough for an easy catch?

3 Stand about 3 metres apart with one foot forwards towards your partner. Try to aim the beanbag to land on your partner's front foot. Keep your own score of good hits.

Group Practices
15 minutes

Partners: with a medium or large ball
One partner will decide on simple ways to travel as a pair with the ball. The other partner will then decide ways to send and receive the ball.

Beanbag among three: piggy in the middle
Two against one, with the two throwing the beanbag to each other to keep it away from the one. Throwers keep moving about 3 metres apart, to give the one a chance.

Small ball each
Practise 'juggling' to keep the ball up, bouncing once in between strikes with different body parts. Move quickly to be ready for the next strike upwards. What is your best score?

Games

Teaching notes and NC guidance
Development over 4 lessons

Warm-up and Footwork Practices

1 The teacher can introduce this activity by having everyone working to his or her rhythm to show that each part is short. 'Ready? All walking . . . all running . . . now jump.' This stops individuals walking or running long distances, instead of getting on with creating a short sequence.

2 Subtraction ability levels in Year 1 should enable pupils to play this game and keep their own score during the 15–20 seconds of each game before the teacher calls 'Stop! Who dodged well and still has five points? Who chased well and caught three or more others?'

Skills Practices: with beanbags

Individual practices

1 From now until the end of the spring term we aim to keep the children moving to keep warm. The throwing and catching of the beanbag, therefore, is done on the move. Most of the teaching is also done while the class is practising. A good demonstration will be very short. 'Watch how Jane looks at the beanbag very closely right into her cupped hands, which are just in front of her eyes.' (10–15 seconds and all start working again.)

2 Throws to low, to medium, and to high give experience in 'feeling' how little or how much effort is needed to produce the varied results. Too much effort is the usual fault.

Partner practices

1 The swing forwards, back, then forwards swing/aim/throw is done with a long, straight arm. Catcher's outstretched and cupped hands give thrower a target to aim at and focus on.

2 Rugby style carrying and throwing with both hands swinging across the body is done almost side by side to ensure easy, successful practice. Beanbag is aimed just ahead of the partner for him or her to run on to.

3 In aiming the beanbag to land on your partner's foot, throw it high enough to cover the distance and try to remember how much force and speed your good ones needed.

Group Practices

Partners: with a medium or large ball

Thinking and *planning* are needed to invent ways to travel with the ball as a pair, and to *send and receive* as a pair. A brief demonstration by the groups after their turn at this activity is recommended because of the important NC requirements being pursued.

Beanbag among three

When the 'piggy' who was in the middle intercepts the beanbag, someone else takes a turn in the middle. The two doing the throwing and catching need to be encouraged to move to the side into a space to be able more easily to receive the next throw.

Small ball each

Start by dropping the ball on to the ground to make it bounce straight upwards. Then hit the ball up with a body part; let it bounce; hit it up; and keep your best score. Five is excellent.

Year 1

Lesson Plan 4 • 30 minutes
December

Emphasis on: *(a) travelling with, sending, and receiving a large ball; (b) responding enthusiastically to challenges.*

Warm-up and Footwork Practices
5 minutes

1   Run freely and change direction when I call 'Change!' Push hard with one foot to make yourself go the other way.

2   Play tag or he with your partner. You may only catch your partner when he or she is not 'safe' on a line (i.e. on a line is untouchable, but encourage regular excursions; change duties often).

Skills Practices: with a large ball
10 minutes

Individual Practices

1   Throw up with both hands, then catch, walking. Aim to throw ball up to about head height and just in front of you for an easy catch just in front of eyes. Hands are cupped ready.

2   Throw ball up and a little bit in front of you to bounce on ground. Run after it and catch with both hands after the bounce.

3   Now show me another way to send the ball a little distance, then collect it and send it again (e.g. kick, head, roll, bounce).

Partner practices

1   Stand about 2 metres apart. Thrower, throw ball slightly to one side of your partner who has to move quickly to collect it.

2   Now use both hands to bounce the ball just in front of your partner for a catch. Make it bounce about 1 metre in front of him or her.

3   Can you invent a standing practice for sending the ball to a partner? Then, try to invent a moving practice for sending it.

Group Practices
15 minutes

Skipping rope each

Skip, running over the rope, one foot after the other. Can the whole group run, skipping, and share your third of the playground 'classroom' sensibly and safely? Leg movements are light but lively. Wrists gently do the turning of the rope.

Partners: with one large ball

Show me how you can send the ball a short distance to each other. I want neat, accurate and successful sending and receiving, please. Variety from a throw to be headed back; from a straight pass to a bounce return; or a kick, fielded and thrown back.

Hoops tag with three chasing seven

Dodgers are 'safe' when sheltering in a hoop. Unadventurous lingering in the hoop is discouraged by the teacher's 'Move! Can you change your direction to avoid being caught? Chasers, remember to touch gently and safely.'

Games

Teaching notes and NC guidance
Development over 4 lessons

Teaching notes and NC guidance
Development over 4 lessons

Games | Year 1 | Lesson 4

Warm-up and Footwork Practices

1   The direction change is produced by stopping your forwards movement with one foot pushing down hard into the ground, then pushing you off in the new direction. The knee of the braking leg bends, then stretches as it pushes you off again.

2   In all our chasing and dodging games we emphasise 'Touch gently to catch others. Hard pushing can cause a fall and a broken wrist or arm.' Emphasise also that we dodge away by sudden changes of footwork, including direction changes.

Skills Practices: with a large ball

Individual practices

1   With slightly bent arms in front, throw up high enough for a catch with two hands at eye level. Restrain the long throwers.

2   Throw; bounce; catch needs judgement and planning to make the ball come up to just the right height for a catch at about waist level.

3   'Sending' has to be sufficiently gentle and restrained to keep the ball from disturbing others or leaving the play area.

Partner practices

1   Passing to one or other side of your partner gives them practice in 'Move early to be standing in position to catch.' This requires careful watching of the ball's height and speed.

2   Hands are spread at sides of ball, with thumbs back and fingers forwards. Arms bend until ball touches chest, then the pass is made by stretching arms to push ball down to bounce just ahead of partner.

3   Class is asked to plan a simple practice to improve and develop the sending of a ball in their chosen way. The same way can be performed for the on-the-spot practice and for the running practice, or they can change the style of the second practice.

Group Practices

Skipping rope each

Running over the rope, skipping, is easy physically, once the skill has been acquired. Because all are moving with ropes flying, they must share the space sensibly and not interrupt the movements of others. Main thoughts can be on the neat, small wrist action used to turn the rope, and on which foot is leading the action in going over the rope each time first.

Partners: with one large ball

In sending the large ball to a partner across a very short distance, we want an impression of neat, well-controlled actions which can be successfully repeated. The receiving is as important as the sending. An interesting development would be for one partner to send the ball one way, and the partner to return it in a different way.

Hoops tag with three chasing seven

Hoops tag is played in one third of the area, using ten hoops as safe havens in which you cannot be caught by the chasers. Those caught take a coloured band and become another chaser.

Lesson Plan 5 • 30 minutes
January

Emphasis on: *(a) working almost non-stop to become and keep warm during winter; (b) practising to improve and remember simple skills.*

Warm-up and Footwork Practices
5 minutes

1   Can you show me some lively, warm-up activities, as you travel around the playground? (Look out for and encourage running, skipping, bouncing, hopping, jumping, slipping sideways, galloping.)

2   Dodge and mark with a partner. Marker runs after the dodging partner, trying to keep within touching distance. On 'Stop!' by teacher all must stop immediately to see who is winner – the dodger who can't be touched or the marker who is within touching distance.

Skills Practices: with a Skipping rope
10 minutes

Individual practices

1   Put rope down, flat on the playground, well away from all others. Can you make a little pattern of jumps from one end to the other (e.g. jump and bounce over; jump and bounce back; stride, stride, stride, stride)? Balance on tiptoes back to the start.

2   Practise skipping freely. If you are just learning, practise stepping over the rope as it slides along the ground, slowly, towards you. Pull it well forwards to hit the ground early.

Partner practices

1   Can you jump over the rope as it circles around, swung low by your partner? Change over after about four jumps.

2   Show your partner a favourite way to use the rope. If your partner skips, watch how he or she uses feet and legs (feet together or apart; one after the other; running; skipping; bouncing; straight or bent legs).

Group Practices
15 minutes

Large ball each

Practise dribbling by hand or foot. If I call 'Stop!' can you control your ball immediately? Use inside, outside and instep of foot for football dribble. Use fingertips for dribble by hand.

Skipping rope each

Can your whole group be aware of one another and try to show me a whole lot of different ways to use a skipping rope? Variety comes from rope on ground and in your hands; on the move and on the spot.

Partners: small ball each

Follow your leader who shows you some simple activities for the other to see and copy. To keep warm, try to keep moving for most of the time. You can throw and catch; dribble with foot or hand.

Games

LIVERPOOL JOHN MOORES UNIVERSITY
LEARNING & INFORMATION SERVICES

Teaching notes and NC guidance
Development over 4 lessons

Warm-up and Footwork Practices

1   The opening activity uses the large leg muscles vigorously as the quickest way to produce body heat. Thereafter, by almost non-stop activity, it is hoped to keep everyone warm. Standing, looking, listening, having long explanations, waiting for noisy children to behave and anything else that inhibits action must be avoided or kept to a minimum.

2   Encourage dodgers to dodge with good direction changes or 'faking' to go one way, then going the opposite way, rather than dangerous, high-speed running away from their pursuing partner.

Skills Practices: with a skipping rope

Individual practices

1   A 'pattern' implies more than one activity to practise the 'joining together with increasing control' requirement in the NC. We want a well-planned, joined-up sequence of activities.

2   Most of the class should be skipping by now and able to keep very active and warm. Beginners will be trying to turn the rope overhead from wide hands to hit the ground in front to make the rope slide towards them to step over.

Partner practices

1   One partner swings the rope around in a big circle, low to the ground for the other to jump over. After three or four turns the one turning the rope must stop to avoid becoming dizzy, and change duties. We want a quiet, neat, high jump from two feet to two feet.

2   We are training pupils' powers of observation and we hope that the observers will praise the work shown by their partners. They should be told to look first for the action and be able to give it a name. Then they look to see how the body parts are working and try to name the actions.

Group Practices

Large ball each

Dribble by hand 'like a basketball player' or by foot 'like a footballer'. With both methods, pupils are asked to keep the ball near enough to them to be able to stop immediately on the teacher's signal. When the teacher moves on to the next group activity, group members can take turns to call 'Stop!' and check the quick control.

Skipping rope each

The skipping group can be the one featured for a short demonstration, each time, before groups change around. We are looking for a group awareness of one another, sharing the space safely and sensibly, and trying to present a varied performance.

Partners: small ball each

In follow the leader, using a small ball, two linked actions, possibly contrasting, would be most pleasing and welcome, particularly if performed in unison. Part of the contrast could be the accompanying actions of the feet, e.g. tiptoe walking balancing ball on hand; then jogging and basketball dribbling.

Lesson Plan 6 • 30 minutes
February

Emphasis on: *(a) performing simple, linked movements; (b) working vigorously to improve learning and to keep warm.*

Warm-up and Footwork Practices
5 minutes

1   Can you run and jump high over the lines? You can push off with one or both feet. Try to use your arms to help balance you, on landing.

2   Keep running and when I call a number, run quickly to join up with others to make a circle with that number in it. Three! (Repeat, calling 'Two!', 'Four!', and probably 'Three!' again.)

Skills Practices: with small balls
10 minutes

Individual practices

1   Make lots of quick little throws and catches to about mid-chest height. Catch with both hands well cupped and fingers pointing forwards.

2   Can you throw the ball up and a little way to one side of you, then run to catch it?

3   Walk forwards, making the ball bounce up well from the ground, and catch it at about head height.

Partner practices

1   One throws to bounce ball to partner (about 3 metres apart), and then the other throws it straight back, without a bounce. Do four then change over.

2   Stand facing each other, about 3 metres apart. Throw up and to one side of your catching partner to make him or her move quickly to receive it.

3   Can you show me a way to send the ball to your partner, while keeping on the move (e.g. walking, side by side, throwing; bouncing in front for a catch; football passing)?

Group Practices
15 minutes

Free practice with a choice of ropes, hoops, bat and ball, large balls

Free practice of a lively activity to improve, and to be able to tell me how you have improved. Make it neat and be able to repeat it.

Small ball between two

Invent a game where one does something with the ball (e.g. counting bounces) while partner races around two markers, then change places.

Partners: beanbag or quoit

Play a lively 1 v 1, throwing to make beanbag or quoit land on ground on partner's side for a point. Decide how many points make a game, then change sides.

Games

Teaching notes and NC guidance
Development over 4 lessons

Warm-up and Footwork Practices

1   In running and jumping high over the lines, emphasise that pupils can run at an angle to a line, rather than always running straight at it, if that gives a better space to jump into. In an upwards jump, the leading leg is bent – with its knee and both arms reaching upwards – when you push off from one foot, as in athletics. We can also jump up high from both feet as in jumping up to head a ball, or show different body shapes in flight.

2   Making a circle quickly is a fun game to practise a quick reaction and response to a signal. The teacher points to the quickest circles made.

Skills Practices: with small balls

Individual practices

1   Partners stand only 2 metres apart and try to throw almost non-stop, aiming at the partner's extended hands which show exactly where the ball is wanted for a quick in and out. 'The ball is hot. How many catches can you make in 30 seconds from . . . now!'

2   From a standing position, throw up to above head height and to 2 or 3 metres to one side of you. Run quickly to catch the ball, standing still, in a good position, with two hands. Watch the ball carefully at all times.

3   With a long arm, bounce the ball down and a little ahead of you to make it bounce up for a catch as you walk on to it.

Partner practices

1   The bounce-throw to land a metre in front of your partner is thrown from shoulder height with one hand. The straight throw is made with a low, straight arm after a preparatory swing back. In both practices the catcher holds both hands forwards to show where to aim.

2   The throw to above partner's head is aimed 2 metres to one side of your partner. This gives the catcher time to run in to position, place the hands correctly, and be still for the catch.

3   Talk about making the receiving easy by sending the ball in a considerate, 'sympathetic' way with as much care as possible.

Group Practices

Free practice with a choice of ropes, hoops, bat and ball, large balls

Whatever implement is chosen must be used for a lively activity to make and demonstrate an obvious improvement. An 'improvement' infers an impression of neatness, control, good use of space, confidence, and even polish and style.

Small ball between two

Planning to invent a game or practice for two requires: a very limited, contained space; an identified activity; a method of scoring; and a main rule to keep the game going and fair.

Partners: beanbag or quoit

'On partner's side' can simply be on the ground on partner's side of one of the paint lines, or preferably on partner's side of a long rope 'net' tied between chairs. Because it is a one-against-one competitive game, both must agree on how to serve, how to score and one main rule to keep the game enjoyable and fair.

Lesson Plan 7 • 30 minutes
March

Emphasis on: *(a) good dodging and chasing; (b) much demonstrating to and learning from a partner and others.*

Warm-up and Footwork Practices
5 minutes

1 Follow your leader, copying the actions being shown. Leaders, can you include some big and lively running and jumping actions, using arms and legs strongly?

2 Chain tag, with several pairs starting off as chasers. When the chains grow to fours with those caught joining on, they split to form two chasing pairs. Winner is last person to be caught.

Skills Practices: with hoops
10 minutes

Individual practices

1 Put your hoop down on the ground well away from all others. Can you run around, showing me different ways to go into and out of all the hoops? (For example, in and land; in and straight out again; in and turn to face a new direction; one foot in to same out; in feet apart; feet in together.)

2 Carefully swing your hoop up in front of you with one hand to catch with two hands close together.

3 Walk beside your rolling hoop and show me how you use your hand to make it keep rolling beside you.

Partner practices

1 Try to show your partner how you can skip using your hoop (e.g. low swings forwards and back, side to side; on a diagonal; or with full swing overhead).

2 Can you bowl your hoop very slowly for your partner to bend and go through?

Group Practices
15 minutes

Large ball among four

In half of your area, play 2 v 2, and score by bouncing the ball in one of the two hoops in your opponent's half. Do not run with the ball. Pass to your partner with two hands for a two-handed catch.

Partners: each with a hoop

Show me some partner activity that you can invent with both working together and able to keep going (e.g. mirroring, while skipping; rolling to each other, throwing up and catching). Hoop can also be on ground for balances.

Bat and small ball each

Practise freely, to 'feel' how gently the bat needs to strike the ball to make it bounce up or down. Use your wrist, not elbow or shoulder. Try balancing it for a few steps, then hit it up.

Games

Teaching notes and NC guidance
Development over 4 lessons

Warm-up and Footwork Practices

1   Follow your leader at a distance of 2 metres so that you can see the actions clearly and the ways that body parts are working (e.g. running with high knees raising and well-bent arms followed by an upwards jump from two feet to two feet with arms stretched sideways to help balance).

2   Start with four pairs as chasers. When caught you join on to the one who caught you. (If game is finished quickly by expert chasers, start with a different set of eight chasers.)

Skills Practices: with hoops

Individual practices

1   Hoops are well spaced out on the ground to give an approach from all sides for a variety of ways into and out again. The variety will include different take-off and landing actions and uses of one, two or alternate feet. Body shapes in the air can vary and a change of direction can take place in the air or on landing.

2   Hoop is swung up with a long, smooth arm action to head height, gently released to carry on a short distance, then caught with both hands and brought down again.

Partner practices

1   If necessary, you can skip, using hoop on the ground, bouncing into and out, or circling around. A low swing with one hand from side to side is the next stage. Two hands can swing it low back and forwards. Both hands can do the difficult swing overhead.

2   This activity needs a 30 or 36 inch (76 or 91 cm) hoop. One partner bowls the hoop slowly forwards towards the partner, who bends to come in from one side to step right through the hoop. An expert partner could try coming in from alternate sides, two or three times.

Group Practices

Large ball among four

Two little games are played in this group's third of the play area. For each game there are four hoops, placed in the corners. Explain to each couple which are 'their' hoops and which are the opponents'. A goal is scored by bouncing the ball in one of the opponents' hoops. The main rule is 'No running with the ball.' The groups can be asked to decide how to re-start after a goal. Groups can also be asked for a rule that helps to keep the game going and fair (e.g. defenders are passive while the ball is being passed, but they become active to stop a scoring attempt).

Partners: each with a hoop

Partner activity in unison with hoops calls for thought and planning, and making allowances for a partner who might be less competent than you. We want something sufficiently simple to allow success and repetition.

Bat and small ball each

Practise with bat and ball, on the move, and try continuous hits upwards; hits up to land and bounce up from the ground; and hits down using bat like a big hand.

Lesson Plan 8 • 30 minutes
April

Emphasis on: *(a) using a variety of implements in a variety of ways; (b) responding to many challenges.*

Warm-up and Footwork Practices
5 minutes

1 In your running, can you find your own nice, easy 'cruising' speed that you could keep going for a long time? Can you 'feel' your running rhythm? One, two, three, four; one, two, three, four.

2 All-against-all tag, counting how many times you are touched, and counting how many others you touch. Be gentle and careful with your touching/catching. No hard, dangerous pushing.

Skills Practices: with a small bat and ball
10 minutes

Individual practices

1 Bat your ball up and keep your best score. Use your wrist, not your elbow or your shoulder as you strike the ball. You do not need to hit it hard.

2 Walk forwards, batting the ball down on to the ground, and keep your best score. Try to bring the ball up to about waist height.

3 Bat it up, let it bounce, bat it up. Strike it gently up and forwards just far enough for you to meet it easily as you walk forwards. As you bat it up, can you be very clever and hit it to a good space where you are not in someone's way?

Partner practices

1 One batting, one bowling gently underarm, can you hit the ball back for your bowling partner to catch? Stand about 3 metres apart only. After six practices, change places.

2 Both using bats, or one with bat and one using hand, play tennis over a line and see if you can keep going (rallying) for three or more hits, which would be excellent. Stand only 3 metres apart.

Group Practices
15 minutes

Partners: with one small ball
Play hand tennis with or against your partner over a line 'net'. Can you make a rally of three or more hits, which would be very good? Take your arm back, ready each time for a long swing.

Bat and small ball each
Practise using forehand and backhand strokes, and some striking up and down, on the spot and moving. 'Feel' how gently you can strike for a good hit.

Follow the leader: choice of ropes, hoops, large balls, beanbags
Try to link two or three ways of using your choice of equipment, and be able to repeat them (e.g. hoop-roll; throw up and catch; spin; or ball-throw and catch; dribble by hand; throw and catch).

Games

Teaching notes and NC guidance
Development over 4 lessons

Warm-up and Footwork Practices

1   Faster than jogging, slower than normal quick running, your 'cruising' speed feels easy. It has a steady, repeating, smooth rhythm.

2   In all-against-all tag, encourage the adventurous chasing after others as being as important as the dodging to avoid chasers. Often, pupils are only concerned with not being caught.

Skills Practices: with a small bat and ball

Individual practices

1   The ball is continually hit gently upwards from a quite high bat, held near head- and eye-level where ball can be closely watched.

2   The hit downwards must be firm enough to bounce the ball up to about waist height for the next hit down. Because you are walking forwards at the same time, the hit must be down and a little way forwards.

3   In the batting up, to allow the ball to bounce up for the next hit you have to judge the amount of force needed, and judge the distance up and forwards to hit it, to let you walk forwards for the next hit.

Partner practices

1   Ball is bounced about 1 metre in front of the batter after a bowl high enough to bounce the ball up to waist height for the return hit. Batter should stand side-on to the bowler, hitting with bat face square to the catcher, who holds hands forwards as a guide and target for batter. By the sixth practice, the batter should be feeling how much force is needed for a good hit.

2   In rallying to each other – at only 3 metres apart to make it easy and controlled – the players must move quickly to stand side-on to where the next return hit will be made. Bat is taken back each time in readiness for the hit.

Group Practices

Partners: with one small ball

In co-operative, one-hand tennis, each player stands 2 metres from the line 'net' and aims to land ball 1 metre in front of partner. This target area can be a chalk circle on each side. Players are asked to try to hit ball to partner's forehand side.

Bat and small ball each

Forehand practice with palm uppermost and backhand hits with knuckles uppermost can be practised by hitting ball straight up using each stroke alternately. Forearm is turned in between. This on-the-spot activity can be alternated with walking, hitting ball down to bounce up ahead of you to waist height.

Follow the leader: choice of ropes, hoops, large balls, beanbags

Joining simple skills together, safely, 'with increasing control', is an expectation within the NC. This should influence pupils' choice of implements for the follow-the-leader activity as they plan and practise linking ways to use them, and to be able to keep on repeating the sequence.

Lesson Plan 9 • 30 minutes
May

Emphasis on: *(a) enjoying the greater variety possible during warmer weather; (b) showing greater confidence and versatility.*

Warm-up and Footwork Practices
5 minutes

1 Run freely and quietly, listening for my shout of 'Change!' when you should suddenly change direction. You do this by using one foot to stop you going the same way and to push you off in a new direction. Right foot would push you to the left, for example.

2 Dodge and mark with a partner. Use good footwork to dodge away from your marking partner. When I call 'Stop!' stop immediately to see who is winner – the dodger who can't be touched, or the marker who can still reach out to touch the dodger. (Change over and repeat.)

Skills Practices: with a skipping rope
10 minutes

Individual practices

1 Can you show me skipping on the move using a running action? Which foot is leading over the rope?

2 Can you skip with feet together using one bounce sometimes, and two bounces sometimes, between each turn of the rope? (Two-bounce double beat for a nice, slow rhythm. One bounce for speed skipping.)

Partner practices

1 Ropes are placed parallel on the ground. With one hand joined, can you balance-walk forwards, backwards and sideways along the two ropes (slowly, feeling for rope, not looking down at it)?

2 Follow your leader at a safe and sensible 3-metre distance, trying to skip in unison using identical actions. Change places.

Group Practices
15 minutes

Quoit between two

Use a long rope, tied between chairs, as a 'net'. Can you win points by making the quoit land on your partner's side of the net? Decide how to serve to start each game. How many points in your game before you change sides?

Partners: with one skipping rope

Can you plan and show me a way that a couple can use one skipping rope? Rope can be on ground or held by one or both. One can swing rope low for other to jump over.

Large ball between two

Send your ball to your partner with two hands, then move to a space for the return pass. Pass; move; and receive, no more than 3 metres apart. Use two-handed chest pass. Move sideways into a space, to keep the 3-metre only gap.

Games

Teaching notes and NC guidance
Development over 4 lessons

Warm-up and Footwork Practices

1 On the teacher's 'Change!' one foot is firmly pressed down on the ground, stopping the forwards movement. The knee of this braking leg is bent and then stretches, pushing you off in the new direction.

2 In dodge and mark with a partner, emphasise that sprinting away from the marker is not wanted. We want good dodging footwork, with changes of direction and speed as good examples. 'Stop!' means stop immediately, or the wrong person appears to be the winner.

Skills Practices: with a skipping rope

Individual practices

1 Running, or walking forwards, stepping over the approaching rope as it slides slowly towards you, is an easy way to skip just after learning. The rope is being turned overhead with an easy wrist action.

2 'One bounce' and 'double bounce' mean one or two beats of the feet on ground between each swing of the rope. One bounce is the quicker, more physically demanding method. Two bounces should be encouraged for general use as it is much easier to keep going.

Partner practices

1 Hands-joined, friendly balancing along parallel ropes has many possible combinations. Both can face the same direction, forwards, sideways or backwards. Each can face a different way. The non-balancing leg and foot can be lifted, stretched and held up in a variety of interesting ways.

2 The 3-metre gap is to prevent the follower's rope going over the head of the leader and causing an accident. A simple running over the rope action with the same leg leading, together, is a spectacular example of partner work.

Group Practices

Quoit between two

Play competitive, 1 v 1 quoits, if pupils are sufficiently skilled in aiming and catching. If not, they should play co-operatively to develop those skills. 'Net' rope should be at about chest height. Aim with one hand and catch with both.

Partners: with one skipping rope

Inventing a way for two to use one skipping rope with good control and success should inspire a great variety of ideas. By putting the rope group on show each time we can extend the class repertoire, which also extends the teacher's repertoire.

Large ball between two

The sending and the receiving are equally important elements to be aware of and practise. A third element of equal importance is the 'move to a new space' after each sending of the ball. By moving to one side and forwards, the players will always be only 2 to 3 metres apart, a distance at which all the practising can be good.

Lesson Plan 10 • 30 minutes
June

Emphasis on: *(a) linking movements together smoothly; (b) co-operating with a partner in a variety of ways.*

Warm-up and Footwork Practices
5 minutes

1 Can you show me the difference between running and jumping long and running and jumping high, over the lines on the playground (straight leading leg with foot leading in long jump; bent leading leg, knee leading in high jump)?

2 Free and caught. Six chasers try to 'catch' others by touching them gently on arms. When caught, stand still with hands on head. Those not caught can free those caught by touching them on the arm. (Change chasing group often.)

Skills Practices: with a small ball
10 minutes

Individual practices

1 Can you bat the ball upwards a little distance with a flat hand? What is your best score? Five is very good.

2 Now use your hand to bat the ball downwards on to the ground. Can you walk about, batting ball down just ahead of you?

3 Can you hold the ball ready in one hand, bat it straight up with the other hand, then catch it with both hands?

Partner practices

1 Bat the ball to your partner with a flat hand. Partner catches it and bats it back to you. The ball is batted from being held ready in the non-batting hand.

2 Stand about 3 to 4 metres apart, with a line or a mark between you to aim at. Try the overhead throw from just above your shoulder, and count your own good hits.

Group Practices
15 minutes

Medium ball among four

Hoop 'chase and hide' with two chasing team players trying to touch two dodgers with ball. Six hoops, well spaced out on ground are 'safe' hiding places where dodgers can't be caught. When both dodgers are caught, teams change duties.

Small ball between two

Aiming and catching at numbered spaces marked with chalk. Try a long, over-arm aiming action, with ball starting above shoulder.

Partners: small bat and ball

Can you invent a simple practice or game that uses bowling and batting? For example, in a small corner, bowl to partner who gently bats it away, and runs to touch corner and back for a point before bowler touches mark. (N.B. Limit the area to a very small space to give fielder a chance.)

Games

Teaching notes and NC guidance
Development over 4 lessons

Warm-up and Footwork Practices

1 Demonstrate with good performers to show what you mean by 'straight leading leg with foot well forwards' in the lively long jump, and the different, more springy, upwards, high jump 'with the leading leg bent'.

2 As in all chasing and catching/touching games, emphasise that the chasers must be gentle in their catching with no hard, dangerous pushing, which could knock someone over and break an arm or a wrist. Encourage good dodging, and trying hard to release some of those caught.

Skills Practices: with a small ball

Individual practices

1 Batting the ball up with a slightly cupped hand is a good preparation for using a bat. Emphasise the gentle, little wrist action with almost no movement in elbow or shoulder. Good footwork is needed to take you to where the ball bounces.

2 Batting down on to the ground and just ahead of you lets you practise 'on the move'. Aim to hit ball hard enough to bounce it up to about waist height.

3 Ball is held in non-striking hand above the hitting hand. Hit is made by bringing striking hand up against the ball to hit it straight up for an easy one-handed catch. Timing of release is the difficult part.

Partner practices

1 At about 2 metres apart, the strike can be gentle and the catch, with both hands, is not too testing. Go for only one hit for a catch rather than the very difficult non-stop rallying to each other, which they will otherwise try with many mis-hits.

2 This aiming at-a-line practice can be tried with a high, over-arm action, starting with the ball above the shoulder of the throwing hand. Catcher stands with both cupped hands reaching well forwards, ready to react to receive the ball. Make it competitive, with one against one, or one pair against the rest.

Group Practices

Medium ball among four

'Hoop chase and hide' is played in half of the third in which the group is playing in and around their six hoops. The two chasers may not run, carrying the ball. They must pass to each other to pursue the dodgers they are trying to touch with the ball.

Small ball between two

Partners stand 4 metres apart. Once again, they use the over-arm action to aim at the numbered spaces to score 1, 2 or 3 points. The competition can be partner against partner, or pair of partners trying to outscore all the other couples.

Partners: small bat and ball

Mini-rounders or cricket, or whatever they agree, must be limited to a tiny part of their area with agreement on the main rule, how to score, how to be 'out' and when to change places.

Lesson Plan 11 • 30 minutes
July

Emphasis on: *(a) demonstrating increasing control over body and implements;*
(b) demonstrating the ability and desire to plan, practise, repeat and improve.

Warm-up and Footwork Practices
5 minutes

1   Follow your leader who will demonstrate a lively sequence of a short walk, a short run and a jump. Watch your partner's feet carefully and see if the two of you can build up to moving in the same way, in unison. (Variety from small or large movements, bent or stretched legs and arms, one or both feet take-off and landing.)

2   Six cross-court sprints. Partners stand side by side down middle of court. On signal 'Go!' both race to touch own side line with one foot and race back to touch partner's hand. (After six times teacher nominates 'First . . . second . . . third . . .')

Skills Practices: with a small bat and ball
10 minutes

Individual practices

1   Can you bat the ball upwards softly to about head height, using your wrist and not your elbow or shoulder as the moving part?

2   Can you repeat this, walking forwards, and try to catch the ball, balanced still, on the bat, every so often? From this balance, start hitting it up again.

3   Can you bat the ball upwards from being held ready in the non-batting hand, let it bounce once, bat it up, then catch it and start again?

Partner practices

1   Batter, strike the ball gently for partner (2 metres away, only) to catch with both hands. Have six goes and change duties.

2   Can you stand side by side, both batting upwards gently? When you have agreed your best team score before one stops, change to both batting down on to ground, again counting your best score.

Group Practices
15 minutes

Skipping rope each

As a group, can you plan to show off many ways to use a rope, including skipping, working alone or with a partner? (Skipping on the spot and moving; feet together and apart, etc.)

One small bat and ball among three

Can you invent a simple little game that uses bowling and batting in a very small space? (2 v 1 batter who must run, when ball is hit, to score runs. Fielders get batter 'out' in agreed ways.)

Partners: one quoit

Rope 'net' tied between chairs. 1 v 1 quoits, trying to make it land on opponent's side for a point. Throw with one hand, catch with two, and aim to deceive your partner by aiming left and right.

Games

Teaching notes and NC guidance
Development over 4 lessons

Warm-up and Footwork Practices

1   'Sequence' means a group of linked actions, smoothly joined to one another. A short walk of about four steps; a short run of about four strides leading into the jump, which can bring the whole sequence to a still finish with a two-footed landing; or the jump can be on to one foot, which starts the next group of walking steps, without stopping.

2   Insist that pupils touch side line, or better still, put their foot down just over the line. If they jump into their turn and land in a crouch 'sprint start' position, facing back towards their partners, the race will be speeded up. About six sprints spread the race out sufficiently to see the winning order, which should be called out, as far as possible.

Skills Practices: with a small bat and ball

Individual practices

1   'Feel' how much effort to put into the hit as you send ball up to about head height only. Hold bat at mid-chest height where you can see ball well. A gentle wrist action is all you need.

2   Walk; hit up several times; catch ball still on bat by going up to meet it coming down, and letting bat 'give' to stop ball bouncing. Hold the balance, then start all over again.

3   Ball is hit upwards from hand as in a table tennis serve. It bounces up, is batted up again, and is then caught with one hand.

Partner practices

1   The batter's short, gentle strike to partner's outstretched and cupped hands, is made from a hit from the hand (as in number 3 in the individual practices), or after dropping the ball to bounce straight up and then hit.

2   Non-stop, co-operative batting: (a) straight up and down between partner and you; is followed by (b) hitting the ball straight down to bounce up between you. One bounce between hits is the target and a 'best score' of six or more deserves encouraging comment, with a demonstration.

Group Practices

Skipping rope each

The group, as a whole, is trying to present a set of varied skipping activities. Such a presentation informs the teacher and the class of the repertoire possible with this implement which can be used in games lessons all year round.

One small bat and ball between three

The bowl, bat, hit, run, field and try to get out simple game must be played in a very limited area, with the batter never allowed to hit the ball hard out of the area. The group needs to agree one main rule for the batter; how to get batter 'out'; and how to change around.

Partners: one quoit

It is helpful to have chalk lines down the side of each little 'court', separating it from the ones beside it. Because the game is competitive, the players need to agree on where to serve from; how to score; and how many points to play for in each game.